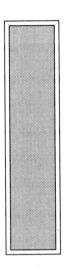

Expressive
Therapy
with
Troubled
Children

ABOUT THE AUTHOR

P. Gussie Klorer, Ph.D., A.T.R., is the Director of the Graduate Art Therapy program at Southern Illinois University at
Edwardsville. She specializes in working with abused children
residing in long-term treatment centers and foster homes. In
her private practice, she works with children, adolescents, and
families with a wide range of problems. She is on the Editorial
Board of *Art Therapy: Journal of the American Art Therapy Association*, and is an invited speaker at colleges and universities across the country. Dr. Klorer is a registered art therapist
and practicing artist, working in mixed media.

Expressive Therapy with Troubled Children

P. GUSSIE KLORER, Ph.D., A.T.R.

JASON ARONSON INC.
Northvale, New Jersey
London

This book was set in 10½ pt. Hiroshige Book by Alpha Graphics of Pittsfield, NH, and printed and bound by Book-mart Press, Inc. of North Bergen, NJ.

Library of Congress Cataloging-in-Publication Data

Klorer, P. Gussie.
    Expressive therapy with troubled children / by P. Gussie Klorer.
       p. cm.
    ISBN 0-7657-0223-1
    1. Art therapy for children.   I. Title.
  RJ505.A7K56 1999
  618.92'891656—dc 21   99-17468

Printed in the United States of America on acid-free paper. For information and catalog write to Jason Aronson Inc., 230 Livingston Street, Northvale, NJ, 07647-1726, or visit our website: www.aronson.com

To the children

whose stories are told

Contents

⦿ *Preface* ⦿

The rainbow is God's promise
Of hope for you and me
And though the clouds hang heavy
And the sun we cannot see
We know above the dark clouds
That fill the stormy sky
A Hope Rainbow will come shining through
When clouds have drifted by.

Ebony, age 13

In my work with children I am amazed, not at how severe their traumas are, but at how resilient the children are. I hear a particularly sad case and think that when I meet the child I will be heartbroken at the severity of his psychological reaction to the horror. More often than not, I find myself struck by his ability to cope and function. This is not to say that the emotional scars are not evident, but often I see that a child's will to survive supersedes another's will to crush the child's spirit. I search for answers in the literature that will help me understand post-traumatic stress disorder, but I learn more from watching the children play and draw.

I came to art therapy because I know the power of using art to express feelings. I may feel compelled to start a painting, but have no idea why. The creative moment comes first, often before I am conscious of what I need to express. When finished with a piece of art, I may write about it, or try to explain its meaning. At each life stage, my art has taken on the qualities of the struggles of that period of time. Through my own art, I learned about process and I learned about myself. Like many artists, I know what it feels like to make cathartic, angry pictures, or pictures that are giddy with color, or lonely pictures that pull inward, so when a client does so I experience kinesthetic empathy. This training in art is an important aspect of training in art therapy.

This book is about more than just art therapy, however.

This book is about children's capacity to heal by means of expressive work and therapy. Many of the children in this book have been horribly abused. These children's stories are painful and at times unbelievable. In therapy, the child is often invested in *not* talking, due to the highly defended nature of the issues, and the child's often excellent coping skills that have helped him to survive. In abuse cases, there may also be a need to protect the perpetrator through silence. Alternative means of expression, without words, are necessary for the child. Expressive therapies that allow for communication of intense feelings are crucial to work with children. Rarely do children draw or enact in play the actual facts of the issues that trouble them. Rather, the issues are enacted symbolically through repetition of themes. Each child develops his or her own symbols and stories. The therapist's job is to help the child find the reparative path through the creative process. For some children it may be through play, for others it may be through art. These are the ways children communicate independently of words.

The reader may be struck by the strength and insight that children are capable of when working creatively in therapy. The key to this work is that it does not rely on verbal processing as the primary means of expression. When words come, it is after the creative expression has taken place. The true work happens when the child creates, when the child's imagery and stories take form, when the child creates a metaphor for the pain and contains it.

The children in this book came to me from several different sources in twenty years of work as an art therapist. Some lived in the residential treatment center where I worked for nine years. Others were living in foster care at the time of treatment and were referred to my private practice by the local child protective services agency. Still others were living in their family of origin, and were referred and brought to therapy by the parent.

Permission to share the children's artwork has been granted by the family court, a representative of the child protective services agency, and/or by the parent or guardian. Quotes from the children are verbatim. Details about the cases have been altered to help disguise the identities of those involved. All names have been changed. I have tried not to change the character of the situation or the child. For ease in reading and in an effort to maintain gender-neutral language, chapters alternate with male and female pronouns.

It is possible, and quite likely, that these cases will be identifiable to the individuals involved, primarily because of the inclusion of the art, which is highly personalized. These cases are shared with respect for the incredible work these children and families have accomplished in therapy, and with the hope that through the work they have done others may be helped. Their stories are shared with love.

⟪ Acknowledgments ⟫

There are many people to thank for their part in the creation of this book. First and foremost, and without whom it could not have been written, are the children and families whose stories are told. I have been enriched by knowing all of them. These children, and many others who are not in the book directly, taught me how important sometimes it is *not* to talk. Bob Baur had the vision to hire the first art therapist at Evangelical Children's Home, where I met a few of the children in this book, and there began my deep love for working with troubled children. The St. Louis County Division of Family Services and the Family Court of St. Louis County supported the concept of this research, and for their permission to use material I am grateful.

I am grateful to Pat Allen and Linda Gantt, two art therapists on my doctoral committee, who saw this book in its earliest stages and provided helpful guidance and support in its conception. Almost as soon as it was written, it began transforming, largely due to the nudge from Cindy Hyden, who saw its potential and had faith in the teaching qualities of the stories. My graduate assistants at Southern Illinois University have provided technical assistance throughout: Sarah Fruehling was a master at literature searches when I needed specific information, and Corey Heimke and Montana Dunkin provided invaluable computer assistance at crucial moments. Diane Rankin, a professional colleague who knew these clients' stories through our bimonthly supervision meetings, provided that objective viewpoint when I needed to talk about cases that were, at times, overwhelming.

Although both of my parents passed away before the book's completion, I thank my parents and family, who put up with me during times when I just worked too much. I am grateful to my friends, who distracted me from my work on more than one occasion, when being distracted was just the thing I needed. And thank you to John, whose unfailing support, friendship, and love make things balanced in my life.

⟪⟨ 1 ⟩⟫

Introduction

Clarissa, age 4, plays in the dollhouse. The theme seldom varies. Children wake from sleep, go downstairs, and the never-ending question is repeated, "Where's mommy? Where's mommy?"

Clarissa was left alone for days at a time to take care of her 1-year-old brother and 2½-year old sister. Few details are available in her record about what her early years were like. Now she is in a foster home. She describes to her foster mother how she used to put water in a baby bottle for her brother and change his diaper. She is highly sexualized, puts dirt and other objects into her vagina, and asks her younger sister to "kiss my booty." She talks to herself often, saying "Bad girl! Bad girl!" She continues to mother her siblings, and initially cannot accept mothering from her foster mother. After a year of therapy, at age 5, she draws a picture of a house that suggests both hope and despair (see

Figure 1–1), and is reflective of her short, chaotic life. She can now reciprocate hugs from her foster mother. She thrives on structure and firmly held boundaries. Her ability to bond again will be crucial to her healing. During therapy sessions, she continues to look out of the window to make sure her foster mother's car is still there.

Working with children is like putting together a puzzle without all of the pieces. We seldom have all the information needed, and we may not know what the picture is supposed to look like. This book delineates some of the complexities of such work and opens the door for further dialogue about how we can best meet treatment needs.

Children often do not have the words to convey their experiences. Therapists must therefore allow children to commu-

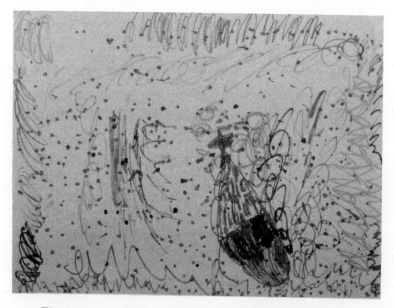

Figure 1–1. Five-year-old's picture of a house

nicate in ways that are more natural for them, primarily through art and play. At each stage of treatment, the child's issues are presented through her creative expressions, independently of her conscious awareness of them or ability to put the feelings into words.

A large number of children in this book have been abused. This is also true of children who are referred to psychiatric hospitals and residential treatment centers, although abuse may not have been the initial reason for referral. Abused and troubled children often develop behavior problems and are then referred for treatment for the acting-out behaviors. Because of the large percentage of children with abuse issues, this will be a primary focus of this book.

Many interrelated variables have an impact upon how children and adolescents process child-abuse treatment issues. Severity and duration of abuse, age of trauma onset, relationship of the perpetrator to the child, defenses and coping skills available to her, and support available from family or significant others all have an impact (Briere and Elliott 1994). Equally important are the child's object relations—her ability to form relationships based upon past experiences. Positive relational experiences, such as the existence of at least one predictable, nurturing person with whom the child has bonded in the past, can greatly influence the extent to which an individual exhibits emotional problems as a result of abuse. A child's ability to bond is a crucial element for psychological healing to take place. Clarissa shows signs of bonding. Her prognosis is good.

The continuum of children's psychological reactions to trauma varies, from little or no psychological disturbance to severely emotionally disturbed. It is erroneous to assume that because a child has been abused she will necessarily have serious psychological problems as a result. A surprising number of abused children cope, survive, and flourish (Beutler et al. 1994). Those who appear to be coping well and who are not exhibiting signs of stress or anxiety may not need to enter therapy at all. Many others can enter therapy at each developmental milestone, attend to the issues at hand, and then terminate until the issues resurface at the next stage.

Others may need years of intensive therapy and/or residential treatment.

Devon plays roughly with the sandtray toys, throwing the army men about and killing them off. He hears a noise outside and stops play immediately. He rushes under the table, crouching down with his head lowered. Although he now lives in a foster home, Devon is hiding from daddy, whom he has not seen for several months. "Daddy is coming to get me," he says fearfully. Devon is also a very bright 4-year-old. He was burned with cigarettes and beaten with a belt as forms of punishment. His parents were suspected drug users, and neglected and physically abused their three children. Devon was reportedly the favored child, but this meant that he was also sexually abused by his mother from an early age. The children were removed from this home and put into a structured and loving foster home. Devon has difficulty containing his behavior and, despite interventions of medication, structure, and therapy, is not able to adjust. Devon's play therapy themes consist of army men and wars, not unlike the play of boys his age, although his story lines are simple, violent, and repetitive. Devon's behavior, including physical aggression toward his foster family, gorging of food,

masturbation, lying, sleeping difficulties, and destructiveness, will not abate. Devon is totally indifferent when his
foster parent enters or leaves the room.

When devising treatment strategies for a Clarissa or a
Devon, the first concern must be to meet the child where he
or she is emotionally. Providing a psychologically safe environment that allows the child to develop his or her style of
communicating is imperative. Creating an environment where
the child can be expressive and where the therapist can then
accurately assess the child is discussed in Chapter 2.

Children often cannot verbalize their experiences, for a multitude of reasons. How does a child put into words the fact that
his mother, the first person he ever loved, the person upon
whom he depends for all of his needs, has just blackened his
eyes and broken his nose? How does an 8-year-old find words
for the sexual excitement, coupled with shame and unbear-
able confusion, when she thinks of her stepfather's late-night
forays into her room? How does a 4-year-old, who does not
understand what death means, find words for the day her
mother shot at her and then killed herself?

These are children who have had adult experiences. There
is no way they can put into words the complexities of emotions and cognitive confusion about what has happened. These
children may be resilient and their defense mechanisms may
have worked well for them. It is not necessarily in their best
interest to break down these defenses and get children to talk.
What is important is that children have a means of expressing the conflict in safe and contained ways. Therefore, they
need alternative means of expression. They need play outlets,
they need to be able to use symbolism, they may need to draw

or paint or create things with their hands because there are no words available. Children may refuse to talk, but rarely do they refuse to draw or play.

Using art in therapy is powerful on several levels. First, the child's symbolic expression is a communication that can be interpreted and that allows the therapist an opportunity to understand and empathize with her. The child's art can be used to assess her level of emotional functioning. Through children's expressive creations in therapy, we can understand their object relations, the developmental tasks at hand, and their coping mechanisms and strengths. The therapist can use the child's art and creative expressions to understand her on a feeling level, without needing to rely upon her verbal skills, memory, or willingness to talk.

Second, the process of creating, in and of itself and *without* interpretation or verbal intervention, can help the child achieve mastery of and resolution for emotional issues. The child takes ownership of a feeling, even if it is not verbalized, when it is expressed through creative means. This is not to suggest that the therapist promote unlimited catharsis, which for children with poor inner controls is countertherapeutic. But when art-making goes beyond throwing of clay and smearing of paint and is redirected and channeled into an art piece that symbolically *contains* the pain rather than merely emotes it, that is where the healing takes place. The resolution on a feeling level can be a tremendous relief to the child. Additionally, the purging of energy that a child can feel after sublimating aggressive or sexual energies into art can be powerful enough to prevent the need for further acting out. Chapter 2 discusses what the therapist can provide to help this work happen.

Chapter 3 presents a dilemma that often arises when working with children. Children learn early how to hide feelings. A mother who is silently grieving a loss communicates to her children that the loss cannot be openly grieved. Parents who do not express anger appropriately teach their children to do the same. Children learn early about family secrets and how to pretend that a feeling or a situation does not exist. The words a child uses often reflect the family's public stance. Yet, her behavior and words may not match what is revealed through the art. We learn to trust the art as a truer measure of what she is feeling because she does not know how to hide feelings in art. In abuse cases, when the perpetrator is a loved (or feared) family member, this can be even more pronounced. The need to protect the perpetrator may be much stronger than the child's need to disclose. Whereas verbally the child denies the abuse and protects the parent, often her art tells the true feeling. We learn to trust her art as a measure of her relationships. How the therapist handles the child's verbal denial will be a crucial part of the therapist–client relationship. Using art as the bridge between what the child says and what she feels will help both therapist and child unravel the complexities of the object relational issues that will be a focal point of treatment.

A premise assumed here is that children process traumatic experiences according to a combination of object relations issues and their stage of emotional and cognitive development. The age of the child at the time of the trauma, the occurrence of dissociation, and the child's present age may all be important in order to understand the child's developmental stage. The age of the child when the trauma happened is important because at each stage of psychological development children develop increasingly sophisticated defense mechanisms that can assist them in coping with trauma. For example, children abused at preverbal ages may become seriously disturbed in their object relations because of the interruption of attachment. On the other hand, children who have made it to adolescence before encountering abuse will have a whole childhood of other kinds of experiences from which to draw, and can activate more sophisticated defenses, and so the severity of trauma may be much less.

Children who are troubled often draw at regressed stages of development (Malchiodi 1990). One can use the artwork to determine the child's level of emotional and cognitive functioning, defenses relied upon, and symbolic messages (Kramer 1971, Levick 1989, Rubin 1978). Chapters 4 through 7 are divided according to developmental stages (Piaget and Inhelder 1969), overlaid with how these are echoed through a child's art development (Lowenfeld and Brittain 1987). A brief description of how the child processes trauma is then included, setting the stage for delineation of more specific treatment issues related to child development and trauma. Case examples and children's art are used to illustrate points. Trauma is an ongoing developmental issue in a survivor's life, and this issue will be processed continually as the child matures into adulthood. At each developmental stage, the child attends to new therapeutic issues, based upon her cognition and normal developmental cycle. A child is only capable of processing treatment issues up to the level at which she is able to function cognitively and emotionally.

Categorizing treatment issues to coincide with developmental stages centers around a desire to get young trauma victims out of therapy as soon as possible so that the treatment does not reflect the therapist's or parent's need to process material at a level the child is not yet capable of. Therapy should resume at the point when the child is ready to process at the next stage. In this way, the therapist is helping both the child and parent see the issues as ongoing, but not all-encompassing. The therapist supports the attachment as well as the individuation of the child, encouraging a practicing period during which she can explore these issues autonomously. There is an implicit hope of promoting the idea of health and a natural progression of treatment, rather than pathology. There is an implied respect for the child's ability to heal through creative expression.

However, in cases where the child's early object relations have been disturbed, particularly in abuse situations where the perpetrator was a primary caretaker and the child is living in foster care, long-term, continuous therapy is to be expected. In cases like these, the therapist may be the only constant object in the child's life, as she moves from foster home to foster home, to residential treatment, to hospital, and has a changing succession of social workers and court-appointed advocates.

A further consideration when working with children is the involvement of the family in treatment. Chapter 8 discusses the integration of individual and family therapy, and how the therapist makes the paradigm shift from one to the other. Included in this chapter is discussion about doing a family assessment with art. The chapter is further subdivided into sections on divorcing families, families experiencing loss issues, court-ordered family therapy, family therapy with an abusive parent and/or the nonoffending parent, and when and if to include a foster or preadoptive family in therapy. In expressive forms of therapy one can attend to issues such as denial, avoidance, or resistance within the family structure.

In Chapters 9 through 13, the focus is on the process of therapy. In analysis of five different case studies, one can see how each child finds a curative path through expressive work, work that is idiosyncratic to that child and cannot be choreographed to be repeated with another child. Each child develops a pattern of creative work that attends to her own issues in a unique way. The therapist's role is to help her find and stay on that curative path.

The book ends with a concluding chapter and an epilogue on countertransference issues. What the therapist does to contain the child's pain so that it does not interfere with the therapist's own life is an important part of this kind of work. This chapter includes discussion about the therapist's inability to always know where the child is going, and the need to hold the ambiguity of not knowing. The therapist must learn to trust the process itself.

Each case is unique, and despite an attempt to categorize some of the treatment issues here, it is understood that ultimately each case truly is its own puzzle, with its own pieces.

✿ 2 ✿

Setting the Stage for Expressive Work

Johnny's first picture in art therapy told much of his story. I told him he could draw anything he wanted. "Anything?" he asked. "Yes, anything." "Anything?" he asked incredulously. I assured him he could draw whatever he liked. "Can I draw a vampire that kills my mom?"

Johnny, age 7, is protective of his mother, and continues to deny all abuse. He entered therapy because his mother had been tying the children to a dog chain outside, and he has permanent rope scars on his neck and wrists. Although Johnny's therapy has not included an admission that his mother hurt him, through art and play therapy he could safely test out his anger toward his mother. Like many of the children in this book, Johnny was referred for physical abuse and neglect. Sexual abuse was a surprise that came later in his treatment, when he began simulating intercourse with his 5-year-old sister on visits. He defended his actions by saying, "You can't tell me what to do. My mother said I could have sex with my sister any time I want!"

Johnny always chose three-dimensional materials to work with, and always entered the therapy room with a plan of what he wanted to make. There was a recurring theme of aggression and a need for protection in Johnny's art pieces. For example, he made a house with toothpicks protruding out of the walls because he wanted it to hurt when someone touched it. When he made dolls in therapy, Johnny pretended that the girl doll was his mother, and then suggested that they were "the kind of dolls that if you do something to them, then that happens to that person. So I can tear the legs off of the mommy doll when I get mad at mommy!" Johnny began repeatedly flying a paper airplane into the mommy doll and laughed every time she got hit.

In a therapeutic environment, children seldom draw or enact in play the actual facts of their traumas. Rather, the issues are enacted symbolically through repetition of themes. Each child develops his or her own symbols and stories. The therapist's job is to provide a psychologically safe environment where the work can happen. An understanding of trauma reactions and post-traumatic stress disorder (PTSD) in children is important. Although most studies on PTSD have been with adults, children involved in intrafamilial abuse are recognized to carry post-traumatic stress symptoms that include chronic affect dysregulation, sleep problems, exaggerated startle response, destructive behavior against self and others, learning disabilities, hypervigilance, dissociative problems, somatization, generalized anxiety, and distortions in concepts about self and others (Famularo et al. 1990, van der Kolk 1994).

Van der Kolk's (1987, 1994, van der Kolk and van der Hart 1991) work in this area suggests that as children mature they shift from primarily sensorimotor activity, to perceptual representations, to symbolic and linguistic modes of organization of experience. When young children are exposed to trauma, the experience cannot be organized on a linguistic level and this failure to arrange the memory in words and symbols leaves it to be organized on a somatosensory or iconic level. Thus it is expressed through somatic sensations, behavioral reenactments, and nightmares. Consequently, it must be approached therapeutically on a somatosensory level as well.

Johnny's 5-year-old sister, Effie, walked into the therapy room and, without saying a word, immediately went to the dollhouse. "This is my brother Johnny," she said as she held up a doll, "and this is my brother Demetrius. This is me. This is our mom cooking breakfast." The dolls ate, then went to bed. She put the Effie doll on the top bunk, one of the brothers on the bottom. On the other side of the room, she put the mother in one bed, and a brother in bed next to her. Then she said, pointing to the two couples, "That's boyfriend and girlfriend, and that's boyfriend and girlfriend." I asked for clarification of who was Johnny and who was Demetrius, and she recanted and said, "No, they not sister and brother. They boyfriend and girlfriend." Effie soon got frustrated with the small dolls and asked if she could use the anatomical dolls. She paired them off, the adult dolls in one bed, and the child dolls in another. The girl doll decided to take off her clothes and take a bath. The boy doll went to the toilet, and as she began her bath, she told him not to look. Later, they went to school and the children had sex behind a building. Their mother caught them and started yelling. The girl started arguing that she is 10 years old and she can do what she wants. The story shifted again. Now the dolls are first-graders, and they take showers and then have sex. When their mother catches them, one says, "I can have sex with my brother any time I want!"

Effie plays frequently with anatomically correct dolls in her therapy. She repeats scenarios of the child dolls having sex and then getting punished for it. She will not talk about her own abuse, but through the dolls she communicates clearly that she is distressed and is trying to understand what she has experienced somatically.

Van der Kolk (1994) suggests that trauma is stored in somatic memory. Traumatized people respond on a behavioral level by avoiding stimuli reminiscent of the trauma, and by becoming emotionally numb. This is punctuated by intermittent hyperarousal in reaction to traumatic stimuli. Johnny, whose general affective state appears limited, becomes aroused easily and acts this out in sexually provocative ways. Van der Kolk suggests that trauma interferes with declarative memory, or conscious recall of the event, but that implicit memory, emotional responses, skills, habits, and sensorimotor sensations related to the experience remain intact. This coincides with Friedrich's (1990) theory of how sexual trauma and sexual acting out are related. From a behavioral perspective, a behavior is likely to be repeated if it is paired with a response that is experienced as pleasurable. Aggression is accompanied by the release of neurotransmitters that reinforce the aggression, which increases the likelihood that the child will engage in aggression again. Similarly, sexual aggression produces satisfaction both from the aggression and the sexual activities. The sexually abused child, having experienced the pleasurable sensation of aggression and sexual activity together, is likely to repeat it. Johnny remembers the sensation of sexual arousal and is stimulated when he sees his 5-year-old sister. His sister, who is known to have been sexually abused by an uncle, is a willing partner. The children are acting out gender-specific roles that have been learned. Effie has developed a sexually provocative prance, and lies down with her legs spread for Johnny. He assumes a more aggressive stance, and simulates intercourse with her. This behavior is dangerous, and sets the children up for further victimization if they do not learn to control the acting out. The therapist needs to work with the foster parents to assure that consequences are given for any sexually inappropriate behavior. The therapist's office, then, becomes the arena where the children can symbolically enact what they cannot talk about and are forbidden to act out with each other.

THE ROLE OF ART IN THERAPY

There are two uses of art in the therapeutic arena. The first is at the assessment phase, when the issues that are troubling the child may not yet be known. This is an area where one should use extreme caution, as interpretation of artwork is much more complicated than a "this means that" relationship. The second use of art is in the treatment phase, when the art is used as a means of working through the issues. This second use of art is the focus of this book because this is where the art can be most beneficial to the client.

It is the contention of this book that children process trauma according to a combination of object relations issues and their stage of cognitive development. However, the age of the child at the time of the trauma and the occurrence of dissociation may be important in order to understand his developmental stage. Because children who are troubled often draw at regressed stages of development (Malchiodi 1990), one can use the artwork to determine the child's level of cognitive and emotional functioning. Lowenfeld and Brittain theorized that children's art is a reflection of their emotional, intellectual, physical, perceptual, social, and creative growth. Art is a logical place to begin when working therapeutically with children, as it provides the therapist with much-needed information, while it allows the child to communicate in a way that is natural for him.

All children progress through a predictable sequence of stages of art development that closely parallels the stages of development outlined by Piaget and Inhelder (1969). The sequence begins with the Scribble Stage, ages 2 to 4; followed by the Preschematic Stage, ages 4 to 7; the Schematic Stage, ages 7 to 9; the Stage of Dawning Realism, ages 9 to 12; and the Pseudo-Naturalistic Stage, ages 12 to adult. The sequence can be accelerated or retarded, depending upon heredity and environmental influences (Lowenfeld and Brittain 1987). The environmental influences are of particular interest to therapists. In the absence of cognitive disability, when a child's art is regressed it can be indicative of emotional stress. The artwork can provide clues as to the child's emotional functioning level, which then offers the therapist a level at which to begin intervention. If a child of 5 is functioning emotionally at the level of a 2-year-old, the intervention should begin at the 2-year-old level.

A therapist trained in art therapy learns a language that is almost completely nonverbal, a language that children speak spontaneously. An art therapist begins as an artist, and understands the language of making art on a very personal level. This means knowing what materials do and understanding how the process of creating taps places deep inside. Understanding the nuances of this nonverbal language and learning how to interpret art takes years of additional training. An art therapist's training includes learning about normal development in art, and then learning how this art development, which reflects both cognitive and emotional growth, is affected by every aspect— strengths as well as weaknesses, positive stimulation as well as negative factors—of an individual's life.

Therapists trained in verbal techniques can successfully borrow techniques from expressive therapies. Therapists should be encouraged to use art with their clients, particularly when the client is *not* talking, because art can help clients begin to talk. Asking the client to draw a picture can trigger associations that may bring him to new awareness. However, deciphering the symbolic meaning in the language requires more training than can be achieved in one book or one workshop on art therapy. A cookbook approach to interpretation is a tempting shortcut, but research shows that this is not a legitimate means of looking at the art.

When using art in treatment, the words should relate to the art process. It is not necessary to go beyond what is in the picture. We speak of "staying with the metaphor," to remind the therapist that often what is expressed in art is not ready to be acknowledged or verbalized consciously. When talking about the picture, the client is really talking about him- or herself anyway. Pushing for ownership of the feelings expressed is not necessary.

In abuse cases, an important aspect to remember when using art in the treatment phase is that the therapist does not need to obtain factual information from the child about what happened. Assuming that the abuse has already been substantiated, the goal of therapy is to help the child overcome the trauma so that it is not an interruption in his ultimate development. The treatment phase of the abuse may include some disclosure, but the emphasis need not be on verbalizing the traumatic incident. Rather, therapy should focus on exploring the feeling component of what happened, and gaining mastery over feelings that are overwhelming for the child.

Trent was a 10-year-old boy in a day treatment facility. He lived in a violent neighborhood, and we strongly suspected that he was being physically abused at home. He was extremely fearful of our calling his parents about his school behavior, and talked about getting whippings with electric cords. Hotline calls were made, but because of the absence of marks when the protective services social worker interviewed him, and his refusal to disclose to the worker, none were substantiated. Trent drew a picture that metaphorically expressed what it was like for him to live in this environment (see Figure 2–1). The picture included a house, and his story was about bugs. He said the children were outside playing and bugs came and started biting and stinging them. The children ran around to get away from the bugs, but the bugs followed them. Then they ran into the house, and the bugs came into the house and kept stinging them. Trent was communicating that the house, which is supposed to be a source

Figure 2–1. Ten-year-old boy's picture of a house

of protection for children, was not adequately protecting him. To ask Trent to take ownership of this feeling may have been premature. However, I expressed empathy by saying, "It must have been terrible for these children not to have a safe place." Identifying with his own metaphor, Trent continued to talk about feelings in association to this picture.

In the same way that a therapist might offer empathic statements during the course of verbal therapy, empathic statements are made about the artwork. A child draws a tornado that is demolishing a town. The therapist might say, "It must be so scary for the people in that town." If the child is communicating metaphorically, in most situations it is not helpful to try to get the client to say it more directly.

When talking to a child about a picture, the best kinds of questions are open-ended. "Tell me about your picture" is a safe beginning. Asking for a title or a story to accompany the picture is helpful. One should not assume that one knows what everything in the picture is. A child of 7 drew a picture that the therapist assumed was a witch. He was annoyed when she commented on it and said, "No, it's not a witch, it's my mom!" Although this may have been an unconscious representation of how he sees his mother, he was not at all ready for this kind of direct interpretation. The therapist would have been much better off saying, "Who is that?" There is nothing wrong with asking a child what something is if one is not sure, and it is much better to ask than to make an erroneous assumption.

There are some definite "don'ts" when talking to a child about a picture. Of these, the most important is not to ask a child *why* he drew something a certain way or used a certain color. We do not want to make children self-conscious about their choices, and a *why* question insinuates that the child may have done something wrong. Making an observational statement will elicit the same information. For example, rather than asking, "Why did you draw that house red?" a therapist might say, "Tell me about that red house." Rather than asking, "Why did you draw yourself next to your dad?" a therapist might say, "I see you drew yourself standing next to your dad." These kinds of statements will help the child notice a particular area of the picture without making him self-conscious about it.

A therapist who attempts to feed interpretations of a picture to a child without the child's input makes a mistake because he needs to come to his own understanding. An interpretation will have much more meaning for the child if it came from within. The therapist can assist children in the quest to understand through carefully worded, open-ended questions that allow them an opportunity to accept or reject a number of possible meanings. Questions about how characters in a picture or story *feel* will help the child to also understand his own feelings. Every aspect of the picture is a self projection. Simply saying, "Can you tell me more? What else is happening? What will happen next?" can bring new information.

RATIONALE FOR EXPRESSIVE THERAPIES WITH CHILDREN

If one is going to intervene at the 2-year-old level, or the 5-year-old level, or even the 10-year-old level, it may be necessary to bypass verbal means of expression initially, and allow the child an opportunity to express himself spontaneously in a modality that is more appropriate to that age. How one chooses which expressive modality depends largely on the therapist's training, but also upon close observation of the child. A therapist will want to observe how he moves into the space of the office, whether rigidly or fluidly. If he is so rigid in movement that he cannot even draw or play spontaneously, the therapist may need to begin with something much safer, say rolling a ball back and forth. Once the child is comfortable in this space, the therapist will want to have him draw, and will notice what developmental stage he draws in. The therapist will also want to observe the child in free play, and see how the play is organized, and will want to see what materials the child gravitates toward. All of these will provide clues to the level and mode of intervention.

The less of a preconceived idea the therapist has about a child, and the more receptive to observation of his interaction with the materials, the better the therapist can meet his needs. For example, one would not assume that an adolescent male would want to play with dolls, but that may be exactly what he needs to do to act out issues that developed at an early age.

> Leroy was a 15-year-old bully, a large young man from the inner city who threatened and intimidated other teenagers. During our therapy sessions, I noticed that he gravitated toward the dollhouse and asked an inordinate number of questions about it. My casual receptivity to his initial interest in the dollhouse cultivated his curiosity further, and I encouraged him to pick up and hold the dolls. One day I said, "You know, we can play with the dollhouse." He was incredulous that I would say such a thing, but in time he developed a ritual of first locking the door to my office "so that no one can just walk in," then turning on the radio so no one could possibly hear, then making us both a cup of tea, and finally getting out the dolls and playing with the dollhouse for the entire therapy hour. The themes centered around nurturance issues. His repeated story was about children asking their mother to cook them food, and the mother refusing to do so. In this environment of safety he was able to express difficult feelings that were far beyond the bravado he expressed outside of therapy.

Children often do not have words for their life stories. Therapy needs to allow them ways to express their fear of attachment, abandonment issues, sexual experiences, and nurturance issues, independent of a reliance on words. Given the opportunity for expressive art and play, the child will frequently act out the issues spontaneously and indirectly. Although the abuse itself may have been erased from consciousness, the nonverbal behavior is very much accessible to the child. Tinnin (1990) speaks of the importance of this nonverbal process, as when one's nonverbal memories conflict with what one consciously remembers. He suggests that when that conflict is troubling to the client, it may be necessary to bypass the obligatory censorship and rescue the nonverbal message in its wordless form. In a nonverbal, symbolic modality, the child is able to reenact and re-create the feelings that accompanied the abuse. It is not necessary for him to verbalize the issues in order for the healing to take place. Rather, through reenactment in art and play therapy he can begin to make sense of what happened at the same nonverbal level where these issues are stored in memory.

THE RELATIONSHIP BETWEEN ART AND PLAY THERAPY

Five-year-old Keith repeated a ritual at the end of every art therapy session of play acting "The Three Little Pigs." I was assigned the role of the big bad wolf and he played the three little pigs. Using the large pillows in my office, he would make a "house" in a corner of my play area, and the wolf would come and huff and puff and blow the house away, sending him scrambling. Finally, on the third or fourth try the wolf could not blow the house down. Keith repeated this theme for several months at the end of each session. There was no need for further intervention from me because the important part seemed to be that he always ended with a house strong enough to counteract the wolf's power. He transferred this theme into art-making, using the same metaphors. He made several houses out of folded paper, which could easily be blown down with a huff and a puff. Then, he made the house "that the wolf couldn't blow down" constructed out of found materials (see Figure 2–2). He used an excess of glue and tape to hold this construction together. The symbolic message appeared to be that his own house had betrayed his need for protection. The repeated theme indicated his need to consolidate the image of a home that would provide safety. His experiments in art helped him to feel his own power. Finally, as he became more convinced of his actual safety in his new home, the stories ceased and he moved on to other themes.

Because the similarities between art and play therapy are numerous, therapists trained in play therapy may find the transition to the use of art a natural occurrence. Both activities rely on a symbolic language developed by the self. Words may enhance the work, but are not necessary. Play and art materials are useful in the reconstruction of the mental representations as well as in the transformation of traumatic visual memories that cannot be easily verbalized. Art and play share the potential of linking the internal and external domains. Both play and art tap into primary process thinking and so allow the child to process the event without the censorship or inhibitions of secondary process thinking (Nader and Pynoos 1991).

Play therapy often includes the reenactment of episodes of an event or the repetition of traumatic themes. Through repetition, the child gains mastery over unpleasant memories and can experiment with new modes of response. Play rituals are often established. These play rituals hold important messages for the therapist, who may not at first understand their meanings. The therapist must be able to tolerate the ambiguity of not knowing. By trusting that the message is important, the therapist may find that the meaning will be revealed in time. During play-therapy enactments, which may be operating on

Figure 2–2. Five-year-old boy's sculpture of "The Three Little Pigs" in the house that the wolf *couldn't* blow down

a symbolic level, the therapist's role is to provide a psychologically safe environment for the expression, and to contain the play behavior.

Similarly, art that is evoked by trauma includes the repetition of traumatic imagery expressed through the child's own schema. In time, through repetition, the child gains mastery over the feelings evoked by the images. The therapist will often not know the meaning, but must tolerate the ambiguity. As the child repeats images or themes in art, the therapist's job is to provide the most effective art materials for this work to happen, hold the images and feelings, and be receptive to their meanings when they become available.

Both art and play allow the child an opportunity to experiment with possible resolutions to problems. He can try on roles and patterns of interaction. It is important that the therapist not add anything to the stories he makes up, which means that the therapist must often change roles with the child. The child projects aspects of the self onto all elements in the story, so there is potential for enactment of many different aspects of the problem within one picture or story.

Ellen and I are playing house. "Now, you be the mother!" she demands. "Okay," I respond. "Well, do something!" she says with annoyance. I do not know how to play this role, however. Does she want a mean mother? A good mother? An absent mother? I can ask her directly, or I can pretend to do something, choosing something completely innocuous, until Ellen directs me further. I choose the innocuous route. "I think I will sit in this chair for awhile" I say as I sit down. This forces the action back to Ellen. Within seconds, Ellen takes charge. "Now you decide to cook dinner . . . now you tell me to get ready for bed . . . now you decide to go out dancing and leave me alone, and I wake up and get scared. . . ." I have never yet met a child who could not choreograph the entire play-therapy scenario. Sometimes the child will give a directive that is ambiguous to me, and then we simply change roles briefly so I can see how to play my part. In this same scenario, Ellen says, "Now you get mad." I have no idea how mad she wants me to get. I tell her to show me how she wants me to get mad. Ellen plays the mother role with glee, as each part in her story is a projection of her own experiences. She wants me to get so mad that I begin to beat my child with a ruler. When we reverse roles again, I simply repeat what she has shown me. Ellen plays all of the parts in her story with ease, and gets even more satisfaction out of doing so. Sometimes Ellen plays too hard, and her blows with the ruler hurt me. I have to remind her that we are only playing.

Children know what they need. A 6-year-old who did not receive adequate nurturing invents a game of "Baby" to ensure that she will be nurtured. A 5-year-old boy develops a play ritual of enacting "The Three Little Pigs" to understand his feelings of lack of safety in his home. Ellen uses play acting to find out what it feels like to beat a child, since she has been beaten so often. Therapists should try not to know too much about what they *think* a child needs, but rather, be receptive to following the child's lead. The child will take the process where he or she needs to go.

PROVIDING A PSYCHOLOGICALLY
SAFE ENVIRONMENT

The therapist needs to provide a psychologically safe environment conducive to the creative process (May 1975). This means a nonjudgmental attitude that allows for playfulness, occasional regression, and experimentation. A psychologically safe environment suggests a permissive atmosphere with firmly imposed limits. A variety of art and play materials should be available. Rules about care and respect for art and play materials and cleaning up afterwards should be clear. Children should not be allowed to leave the therapy room in disarray. Their entire lives have been in disarray; it is important that they begin to learn that after destruction there is a return to order. Five or ten minutes at the end of a session devoted to cleaning up and returning order actually is empowering for the child. It is a part of the therapy process not to be overlooked.

The beginning of the relationship in expressive therapy sets the tone for the work that will follow. The first time a child enters therapy, the therapist has usually talked to his social worker, parent, or guardian, and has some idea of what the issues are that will be the focus of treatment. When meeting the child for the first time, the first question might be to ask him if he likes to play and do art. Invariably, he nods or answers yes, and is willing to come into the office. This is not a ploy. Children always do art and/or play when they come to therapy, as this is the primary work in expressive therapy. Most expressive therapists begin with some kind of assessment, which will not be typical of later sessions, so this should be explained by telling the child that today he will be asked to draw certain pictures, but in future sessions he will do all of the choosing. The assessment usually includes three or four directed drawings, chosen because of the child's particular history or issues. It is useful to begin with a free-choice picture, in order to assess how the child presents himself in new situations. There are a number of standardized drawing assessments that are used by art therapists, including the House-Tree-Person-Person (Buck 1985, Hammer 1958), Kinetic Family Drawing (Burns 1987), Ulman Diagnostic (Ulman 1977), Levick Emotional and Cognitive Art Therapy Assessment (Levick 1983), Silver Drawing Test (Silver 1990), Formal Elements Art Therapy Scale (Gantt and Tabone 1998), and others. Some therapists combine elements of these and make up their own series.

Once finished with the drawing evaluation, some play time should be allowed, along with a tour of the art room and of all the art and play materials available. The goal of Session 1 is simply to get the child to want to come back for Session 2. At this point, the therapist wants to entice the child with the creative possibilities available. The therapist will want to ask him why he is coming to therapy, so as to understand his perception and what he has been told.

After the first session, the therapist will want to encourage the child to choose materials to work with. When a child is too timid or stuck to choose, the therapist may have to choose at first, picking a range of materials in successive weeks and exposing him to as much variety as possible, so that he will begin to experience how the different media feel. Inevitably, the child will like some media more than others, and this usually leads to his becoming more assertive in choosing. The child's material choices are always significant, and can tell the therapist about his comfort level, coping skills, and strengths.

The relationship established in the course of therapy is itself one of the curative factors. The child enters the relationship tentatively, having no reason to trust this person, based on his past experiences of abuse, lies, and disappointments. Therefore, the boundaries that are set, the rules of the art room, and the consistency of the time and place of the meeting are concrete ways that the child begins to learn to trust. If possible, one should see children on the same day at the same time each week. This allows them the opportunity to predict, and hence anticipate, therapy sessions. It is imperative that the therapist stay consistent with starting and ending times, and not be late, as timeliness is one of the first ways children learn that they are important in the eyes of the therapist.

The process of letting children make the decisions about what activities to do and in what order encourages them to develop their own therapy rituals. This predictability helps to make the session safe. As the child becomes more comfortable with the therapist and the setting, the relationship begins to change. Whereas at first, he is content to have the therapist watch him do art, at a certain point many children seek more interaction. They may assign the therapist the role of "helper" during the art process, saying things like, "Now you hold this . . . Now you take that brush and clean it, while I use this one." In play therapy, the child begins to assign the therapist roles to play. When this begins to happen, as in the case of Ellen, a crucial point is that the therapist must resist any notion of adding anything new to the story that the child develops. Ultimately, the child plays all the roles in his story, and the story belongs entirely to him.

As the relationship develops, the therapist will begin to get to know the child through his expressions and choices. It is important to take scrupulous process notes, both during and after the session. The therapist must pay careful attention to detail in expressive therapy sessions, as the nuances of symbols can easily be overlooked, and if one doesn't write down all themes that come up in the order in which they are presented it is easy to miss a subtle pattern or change. Writing process notes while actively engaged in play or art can be tough, but jotting just a few phrases will jog the memory later, when there is more time to write details. The process notes should include the order in which the child engages in the choices, what materials are chosen, what his reactions to the materials are, all themes or stories that are developed, any pertinent verbalizations while engaged in the process, and his emotional reaction to the session. Through careful note taking, the therapist will get to know the child's themes. The themes will change in relation to stressful events in the child's life, and the therapist will begin to understand how he is coping with the stress.

Within the session, even chaotic discharge should be handled in a controlled manner so that the process is not over-whelming to the child. The child does not have a firmly de-fined ego, so the therapist needs to be the supportive force that will not allow his impulses to take over in a destructive man-ner. For example, wedging of clay to get the air bubbles out before using it can sometimes lead to throwing of clay. Begin-ning therapists sometimes mistakenly believe that throwing clay is always cathartic, and hence beneficial. However, there are media that invite regression, and these should be used with caution, especially with children. Although throwing clay may be cathartic, for children who are acting out aggressively, *con-taining* impulses is the goal, not exploding. Therefore, the thera-pist needs to teach the child how to wedge the clay in a con-tained manner, which teaches him respect for the medium, while allowing for controlled expression of anger. The child will feel secure knowing that creativity is possible, but total destruc-tion is not. This is a good metaphor for containing the child's own behavior. It is frightening for children when they are so out of control that they need to be restrained in order to keep them from hurting themselves or others. Teaching children to control their outbursts is metaphorically done each time the child learns to contain angry impulses with art materials.

Children will be drawn toward materials that "fit" with the expression they need to make. Whenever possible, the child should choose these materials. Children who need structure and control often reject a medium such as paint, which is dif-ficult to control, in favor of markers or pencils. Some children fear tactile media, such as clay, while others gravitate toward it because it best suits the kind of emotional release they need to make.

Understanding the properties art media have is an important part of creating the therapy environment. Unless one has first-hand knowledge of a particular medium and its potential effects on clients, it is best to stay with basic media, such as oil pastels, markers, and crayons.

Ideally, in individual therapy the therapist should not be too directive with the art. Given the opportunity to spontaneously create without imposed directives, children will develop recurring themes. Once a theme is repeated consistently, the therapist may be assured that some working through is occurring. At this level, an art therapist may suggest a new medium that will enhance the child's expression of a particular theme. However, careful attention must be paid to media selection, because a material that is not suited to a particular child's developmental stage or temperament may leave the child frustrated and thwarted in his attempts. The right medium, on the other hand, may provide the stimulus for true sublimation.

Through the free creation of art, children will develop recurring symbols with idiosyncratic meanings related to their issues. These symbols are not transferable from one child to the next, although there can be similarities. When a child has come up with something of urgency that he or she must create, it becomes the therapist's responsibility to ensure that the child can be successful by providing materials that will make it possible.

In group art therapy, on the other hand, structuring the session for the children is imperative. The therapist may need to assign art directives centering around the group's common issues. This can alleviate some of the anxiety associated with group process and lead to more successful behavior management within a group context.

SUBLIMATION IN ART THERAPY

Sublimation in art is that moment when the art process becomes healing, in and of itself. Unlike the emotional discharge seen in cathartic work, in sublimation the image becomes more contained. Aggressive and sexual energy are neutralized (Kramer 1971). The artwork symbolizes the emotion, but the emotion is not acted out. When a therapist is working with the child toward sublimation, the therapist must be totally attuned to his material needs. He will be absorbed in the art process, and may need support on several different levels, emotional and well as structural. When necessary, the therapist must be able to assist with the art materials technically, so that the expression is not too frustrating for the child's less developed art skills. There can be tense moments. However, according to Kramer (1971), an essential feature of sublimation is the great amount of genuine pleasure the activity provides for the child.

An example of sublimation can be seen in Figure 2–3, a three-dimensional life-sized self-portrait by 16-year-old Tiara.

Prior to this painting, Tiara had been unfocused with her art, producing eighteen by twenty-four inch paintings that were typical of adolescent discharge—blobs of undifferentiated color, chaotic, angry, and unfocused. She was not invested in this art, and was bored by it, but did not seem to know how to focus her energies. Tiara was experiencing the dilemma that many adolescents in residential treatment experience. Developmentally, she was supposed to be rebelling against parental authority so that she could differentiate and separate from it. However, since she was living in a resi-

Figure 2–3. Sixteen-year-old's life-sized self-portrait

dential setting, this was not possible. Often, adolescents in this situation turn their rebellious anger against themselves.

I had been preparing a slide presentation of client art, and slides were on my desk when Tiara came in. She asked to view the slides. I hand-picked a few that might stimulate her artistically, feeling that she was stuck in her art making and hoping that it might challenge her creativity. Tiara was drawn toward a technique of mask making, and suddenly felt challenged to do something much larger and more monumental than her previous work. She wanted to do a life-sized self-portrait that would appear as if she were stepping out of a mirror, from another dimension, into reality. Tiara became totally absorbed in the making of this portrait. It was not without its tense moments. Her first plan was to do the mask in plaster. I explained the process thoroughly so Tiara would understand all of the implications inherent in this kind of work. Mask making out of plaster requires a well-established level of trust between therapist and client. We arranged for a two-hour session on an Open Studio day, as the process is quite time-consuming. We first made a rubber mask of her face out of plastic moulage, then covered it with plaster. Unfortunately, the plaster was not a perfect consistency, and a friend of hers entered the room as Tiara was lying on the art room table with breathing straws peeking out of a plaster cast on her head. The friend started laughing, Tiara started laughing, and the sculpture was ruined because it had not yet set. Undaunted by this failure, Tiara insisted that we try again. This time, we used plaster gauze, a technique that results in less detail on the mask but that is a much simpler process. Once the face mask and her arm cast were complete, she worked for over a month on the rest of the project. Tiara wanted everyone in the treatment center to see it in process, and she often brought in her social worker, teachers, and friends so they could comment on her progress. All decisions were made by Tiara, with technical assistance offered only occasionally. She became more creative and daring as the piece progressed, adding one of her own shoes and a pair of jeans to enhance the reality component she was looking for. The pride she felt when she was finished came from deep within. This piece of art, with its "anarchy" theme, offered her an opportunity to express her need to rebel and form an autonomous identity. It is interesting to note that she did not continue to do art once this piece was finished. She began dabbling again, with little focus. It may be that in this one piece she contained and sublimated the aggressive and sexual drives that are so typical of adolescence. She did not have a need to continue the process beyond this monumental expression.

The beauty of art is that it is a haven away from consciousness. Tiara created this piece at the moment that she needed to do so, and then moved on to the business of adolescence, becoming an autonomous individual. The art offered her a place to think, practice, create, play, sublimate. The process of creating, in and of itself, was therapeutic for her. We did not need to verbally process this event in great detail. She took the sculpture-painting and displayed it in her room, where she could revisit the issues in her own time.

◖◒ 3 ◓◗

"Daddy Beat My Sister, Not Me": Trusting the Art More Than the Words

David, a 13-year-old boy in residential treatment, had an endearing smile and made easy friendships with peers and staff alike. Like the other boys his age, David liked to dance like Michael Jackson and goof off with his friends. He would not wear shorts or a swimsuit in the summer because he did not want the burn scars on his legs to show, but aside from that there were no tell-tale signs that David was anything other than a normal child who happened to live in a children's home. David would excitedly anticipate his visits with his mother in jail every other month. Their reunions would be tender expressions of affection as they planned the house they would have when she was released. They would play games and laugh and talk for the entire hour. David's mother was in jail because she would pour boiling water on his legs when he was bad. David would physically attack anyone who said anything bad about his mother.

Valerie, age 10, always talked about her mother coming to get her from the children's home in which she had lived for several years. Valerie, too, was defensive if someone said anything derogatory about her mother. When Valerie was 4, her mother used a razor blade to slice over one hundred inch-long cuts into Valerie's once pretty face.

Jason was found abandoned in a field at age 10 months, malnourished, unclothed, and covered with insect bites. He had developed the traits of infantile autism, and was completely withdrawn into himself until his mother resurfaced one day, whereupon he became suddenly alert and excitedly responded to her.

Children who have been abused are often protective of the abusive parent, deny the abuse, and long to be reunited with the abuser, even when that means inevitable further abuse. If the child has formed an attachment to the abuser, that attachment is stronger than her fear of pain.

The first relationship of a child's life sets the stage for her future relationships. If that first object is loving, consistent, and nurturing, the child develops self-worth, confidence, and the ability to love back. If that first object is selfish, sends mixed messages, and is abusive, the child may continually be drawn toward that person, seeking out love, but in the process learns that it is dangerous to trust or to love again.

Children experience a desperate need to protect themselves from the terrifying reality of the parent's destructiveness. Were the child to acknowledge this consciously, it would awaken fears of annihilation that would endanger her psychological survival (Green 1985). Consequently, the child denies the abuse and defends the abuser. A therapist needs to understand the normalcy of this reaction, and knowing how to work with it, both cognitively and emotionally, is imperative. Object relations and attachment theories help the therapist conceptualize treatment in relation to these issues. Crucial to attachment theory is the work of Bowlby (1969, 1973), who studied attachment behavior in both human and animal relationships. Bowlby's (1973) principal thesis is that whether a child or adult is in a state of security, anxiety, or distress is determined to a large degree by the accessibility and responsiveness of his or her principal attachment figure. Bowlby's ethnological research suggests that in conditions where the attachment figure also elicits fear, both human and nonhuman creatures are likely to cling to the threatening or hostile figure rather than run away. Citing Cairns's (1966a,b) experiments with lambs, Bowlby (1969) describes a lamb and a dog kept together in a cage without restraint, where the dog mauled, bit, and abused the lamb. Despite this, when the pair were separated, the lamb continued to seek out the dog for companionship. In the same way, abused children seek out the abusive parent.

When the abuser has been a primary caretaker and one with whom the child has formed an initial attachment, the emotional destruction caused is far greater than the physical pain. The child will continually stay involved emotionally, and continually be hurt and disappointed.

For the abused child, this can result in denial of abuse and a protective stance toward the parent. The child's inability to see the parent as abusive, in the face of sometimes striking evidence, can be a difficult hurdle to pass in therapy. Treatment when the child is denying the abuse is particularly delicate, because the therapist's relationship with her may be tested through the therapist's handling of this untruth. The child's need to protect herself from the feelings associated with the abuse may prevent her from allowing it to come into consciousness.

Children may deny the abuse verbally but often another picture is told through their art.

> Figure 3–1 is a picture drawn by a 10-year-old girl. It began as the portrait of her mother, and then turned into an angry and aggressive-looking dog. When I asked the child about the picture, she said it was a "happy" picture. The denial in her case was such that she could not see this as a projection of her feelings toward her mother's abandonment of her, and it would have been inappropriate to suggest it. Her mother had identified Linda as "the problem" in the family, and placed her in a residential treatment center. Linda accepted this role, and continually said she would be good if she could go home. Her mother's inconsistent visitation set Linda up for temperamental outbursts and physical aggression that ensured she would not be discharged. It was not until many months after completion of this picture, after working on simple identification of feelings (which was difficult for Linda), that we could even begin to approach the issue of her relationship with her mother.

If simple denial is not enough to protect the child, a more sophisticated defense, that of splitting, may need to be activated. Fairbairn (1941) explains how the abused child uses splitting to cope with the abuse. Because of the complex psychological process of attachment and separation-individuation

Figure 3–1. Ten-year-old's portrait of her mother

that occurs in a child's earliest years of life, if an attachment has been made the child who is abused cannot reconcile the idea that the parent, whom she loves, can also be an abuser. The child's intense need for an object means that even a bad object is better than no object at all, for abandonment is a much greater fear. Children with an abusive parent will do anything to hang on to that parent, including being compliant in receiving abuse (Scharff and Scharff 1994).

It is intolerable to the child that the parent is bad, so she needs to split the good and bad aspects of the abuser and the self. In order to tolerate the abuse and make sense of it happening, the child takes on the qualities of the bad object, preserving the abuser as the good object (Fairbairn 1941, Seinfeld 1989, St. Clair 1986). In believing that she provoked the abuser by her badness, the child can have the illusion that if only she were to become good then the parent would stop the abuse (Seinfeld 1989). Thus children take on the qualities of the bad object and will compliantly take on the abuse rather than risk losing the parent as an object, which, to a child, is akin to dissolution of the self. This defensive coping strategy, which necessitates a continued attachment to the abusing parent, affects the child's self-esteem, keeps the child at risk for future abusive relationships, and results in a regressive pull toward the abuser, despite the emotional and physical pain that is associated with him or her. Additionally, by becoming the "bad" object, the child gains a sense of control over both the timing and the anxiety associated with the abuse (Green 1985, Tuohy 1987).

Children who have been abused rarely have the strength to break from this pull toward the abuser, particularly if the abuser remains in contact. The child's hope is that, if only she can please the parent, the parent will love her. But of course, the child can never please the parent. The scene is all too familiar to those working in residential treatment centers: the child waits on Christmas day for mother to visit, but mother never comes. The child acts out in anger. However, before the child can accumulate enough of these rejections to begin to hate the mother, the mother emerges one day full of promises and smiles, telling her how much she loves her. This scenario of mixed messages is one of the most destructive for children, for it keeps their hope alive, keeps them involved in the relationship, and keeps them from forming a new attachment.

The purpose of splitting is to cut off the bad object so that the child does not feel the intolerable pain of rejection from the parent. According to Fairbairn (1941), splitting and repression always occur together. Splitting allows the child to maintain a conscious relationship with a good object while maintaining a relationship with the bad object in the unconscious. The part of the ego that relates to the bad part of the object is split off and repressed along with it (Scharff and Scharff 1994).

> Five-year-old Michael did not dissociate the event. He recalled details of the morning of his sister's murder with complete accuracy and was able to identify appropriate feeling states in association to her death. However, neither he nor any of his five siblings could blame their father, who was in prison for the murder. During the entire first year of therapy the children drew happy pictures of their father as a part of the family, and sent the pictures they made to their father in jail. When asked directly about abuse at home, Michael denied that his father ever whipped him. "Daddy beat my sister, not me," he said. He denied this even in a family session when his older brother contradicted him and reminded him of a beating he had received when he was 3. Michael's response was to put his head on the table as this was discussed. He appeared sad. I said, "Michael, sometimes our mind doesn't want to remember things that hurt us and make us sad, so our mind makes us forget, but that doesn't mean

it didn't really happen—it just means we can't remember it right now." Michael's identification with and need to protect his father was too great to include the memory of his own abuse. Had he been abused, then he too could die. His denial allowed him to preserve the image of a father who loved him. Michael began taking on more characteristics of a "bad" child, getting in trouble in school and exhibiting severe aggressive behavior, including taking a knife to school to kill another child. Michael's siblings were also invested in the denial, although, unlike Michael, they had not witnessed the murder. His 9-year-old sister, Karen, epitomized her denial when I asked her to draw a picture of herself (see Figure 3–2). In this picture she drew herself and her murdered sister jumping rope, as if nothing had happened.

Figure 3–2. Nine-year-old's self-portrait, including herself and her murdered sister

Crucial to the work with this family was work with the mother, for until she could model for the children an acknowledgment of the two sides to her husband, it would not be safe for the children to see his abusing side. An aunt, who was a strong support for the entire family, was also brought into the therapy. Many sessions were spent exploring the two sides of the perpetrator. In a family session that included the aunt, the directive given was for each family member to draw a picture of the children's father. Karen initially drew Figure 3–3, reflecting once again her denial. She wrote, "I love you daddy, O.K., You better be sorry, O.K., I am sorry. O.K., I love you mom, O.K., I love you man, Bad boy, O.K." Notice how as soon as she wrote each negative statement, she "fixed" it by saying "O.K." or "I am sorry." The anxious

Figure 3–3. Nine-year-old's first picture of her father (perpetrator)

quality of her lines betrays the actual feelings she cannot, at this moment, face.

Karen's Auntie, less close to the situation and therefore not invested in the denial, drew Figure 3–4. Clearly, her aunt had strong feelings about her brother-in-law, and was not afraid to express them.

As soon as Karen saw her aunt's picture, Karen looked to see her mother's reaction and then quickly took another piece of paper and drew Figure 3–5. This was in dramatic contrast to all previous, happy pictures. It was a totally non-verbal communication, but for the first time her aunt and her mother had given her permission to feel these feelings. In this

Figure 3–4. Auntie's picture of the 9-year-old's father (perpetrator)

I feel ANGAY with MY DAD

DENIE

FOR What he DONE

Figure 3–5. Nine-year-old's second picture of her father (perpetrator)

picture, Karen has borrowed images from her aunt's picture, expressive of her own repressed and split-off feelings.

Denial may be an active response, as experienced through splitting and repression, or passively experienced, as in dissociation. In either active or passive denial, it is important that the therapist stay with the child's denial. It is counterproductive to attempt to get the child to disclose, because the therapist's relationship with her is far more important. These defenses helped the child to survive the ordeal and cannot be broken down easily. Nonetheless, factual information must be presented whenever possible to help the child see the reality.

Dissociation, according to Scharff and Scharff (1994), occurs when the child feels overwhelmed and repression itself fails under the impact of the abuse. In dissociation, the child enters a trance-like state of numbness that secures her survival and makes tolerable the pain and fear.

The severity of the syndrome is proportional to the duration of the trauma and the age of the child at trauma onset (van der Kolk 1994). Victims of ongoing abuse appear significantly more disturbed, with symptoms ranging from depression to psychosis, than do children reacting to a single event of abuse (Kiser et al. 1991). Dissociation is characterized by the child's ability to store traumatic memory in an alternate state of consciousness. Dissociation of a traumatic experience occurs as the child is experiencing the event (van der Kolk and van der Hart 1991) wherein the child splits off the memory and the affect that accompanies it, and becomes numb to both memory and experience. The most severe reactions of dissociation occur when the abuse is frequent, unpredictable, inconsistent, and the child has been exposed to some form of love (Braun and Sachs 1985).

An example of the more passive form of denial seen in dissociation can be observed in the case of Bonnie, an 8-year-old child in treatment (Klorer 1995).

> Bonnie's sexual and physical abuse by her mother and her mother's boyfriend before she was 5 was substantiated by physical evidence. She had a venereal disease at age 6. She had bowel problems and a lack of control over her anal muscles, problems that were suspected to be the result of the sexual abuse. Bonnie continually denied that she had been sexually abused, and talked about wanting to live with her mother, not unlike many children in residential treatment. Her strong denial system made treatment difficult. She adamantly refused to acknowledge that anything had hap-

pened, despite medical evidence and sexual-acting out be-havior that suggested otherwise. Her pictures in art therapy were frequently phallic-shaped objects that were painful to look at. One example is shown in Figure 3–6, which was meant to be a picture of a baby bottle.

In Bonnie's therapy, play rituals were developed with anatomically correct dolls. A relationship of trust that al-lowed for uninhibited play therapy had already been estab-lished. I introduced the dolls to Bonnie in a casual manner,

Figure 3–6. Eight-year-old's picture of a baby bottle

along with other play therapy props. It appeared that Bonnie chose to use the dolls because they tapped into the unconscious issues that she was working with in therapy. Bonnie created a ritual with the dolls surprisingly quickly. Using pillows and sheets, she made a clubhouse under my desk. She instructed me to crawl under the sheet to get inside, and she would also crawl under, after turning down the lights to make the environment more psychologically safe. Once protected under the desk, Bonnie would play with the dolls, taking the role of "teacher." She took the female dolls for herself and gave the male dolls to me. Bonnie would undress the females and position the mother doll fondling or performing oral sex on the younger doll. "This is what mothers do with their daughters," she would announce. "Now you show me what fathers do with their boys." I would feign ignorance so that Bonnie would have to take the male dolls and demonstrate what fathers do. Each week Bonnie would give me a lesson and a test. I continually feigned forgetfulness so that Bonnie had to do all the manipulating of the dolls. This game would be repeated for most of the hour. The compulsion to repeat the story lasted for many weeks. Bonnie appeared to be processing her own abuse, although she still would not discuss it. Processing took the form of teaching Bonnie about appropriate and nonappropriate touch. The last few minutes of each session, after all the pillows and sheets were put away and we were sitting at a table, were spent reframing the activities for Bonnie in a new way: it is not okay for mothers to touch their daughters' private parts in that way; it is not really okay for a man to put his mouth on a child's private parts; adults should not do these things with children.

Bonnie's therapy, which progressed on both of these levels, did not lead to disclosure of her own abuse. Her need to protect the image of a good mother was too strong. Bonnie likely had dissociated her abuse, and hence the dolls offered the opportunity for abreactive work that was important in order for Bonnie to gain mastery over her nonverbal memories of abuse.

In both of these examples denial is an important defense for the child. In object relations terms, the therapist's role is to create the kind of holding environment that will allow the child to explore both verbal and nonverbal memories and feelings without censorship. The therapist must be able to tolerate the ambiguity of not necessarily knowing what happened to the child. By creating a psychologically safe environment to contain the play behavior (or the art, or the expressive movement), the therapist provides the child an opportunity to reenact, re-experience, and reprocess the event.

APPROACHING CHILDREN'S DENIAL THROUGH CREATIVE MEANS

The artwork a child makes is often a clue for therapists and can reveal more than the child is able to understand or acknowledge consciously, although it is obvious that denial can be held in the artwork, as Karen attempted to do in her early attempts. However, she could not keep up this facade, and her artwork showed signs of anxiousness in the line quality and her compulsion to negate, until she was finally able to produce Figure 3–5. In Bonnie's case, her play behavior repeated abusive scenarios that she could not talk about, and her images continually reflected painful phallic figures that suggested extreme anxiety in regard to sexuality, despite her lack of memory and denial.

In many instances when a child is denying abuse, the picture she draws can tell the therapist about a whole different world of experiences and feelings. A therapist will want to be keenly attuned to what the child is drawing as well as to what she is *not* drawing. It is crucially important that the therapist stay at the level that the child is willing to verbalize, rather than trying to process with her what is being expressed through art or play. Robbins (1987) talks about art's ability to penetrate defenses at the same time that the client remains unable to assimilate the inner meaning of the metaphor in conscious awareness. The art form mirrors the object relations back to the client. The therapist must be careful not to overwhelm the client with words that are too difficult for him or her to assimilate, keeping a constant assessment of the client's defenses. It is counterproductive and nontherapeutic to confront children with what is revealed in the images, but it does give the therapist information that helps to assess the severity of the trauma and to determine the direction of treatment.

For the child, the truth is often held in the art. Trust the art first—it does not lie.

TREATMENT CONSIDERATIONS IN CHILD SEXUAL ABUSE CASES

Before proceeding with categorizing children into developmental stages and outlining treatment issues, a few caveats need to be stated. Because every situation is different, a phenomenological approach to treatment is necessary. Every child is unique in terms of what happened, what coping skills were available, and what the early object relations were like, as well as in cognitive ability, defenses used, longevity and severity of abuse suffered, and support available from family or significant others. There are no set treatment goals that will be appropriate for every child. However, one can and perhaps should look at what the child is capable of processing developmentally, and this *can* be categorized. One needs to take into account how the child is functioning on a cognitive as well as emotional level, as this may help direct the course of treatment and suggest possible approaches.

Any attempt to categorize children into developmental stages for treatment must first look at the severity and duration of the abuse. A child who was digitally fondled by a baby-sitter on one occasion cannot easily be compared to a child who was repeatedly seduced by her father. The relationship of betrayal and confusion that an incestuous contact evokes causes myriad complicated treatment issues and activates object relations responses that far exceed the reaction in the former example. In the same vein, a child whose abuse entailed gradual seduction by another child would appear to suffer less trauma than someone who was brutally anally raped.

Generally, sexual abuse involving intercourse is more traumatic than fondling, and one of the most prominent factors leading to trauma is the use of force (Walker 1988). There are many instances of abuse that will not cause long-lasting trauma, and one or two sessions focused on prevention may be all that the child needs (Gomes-Schwartz et al. 1985). Further therapy would only serve to further traumatize the child and is often reflective of the therapist's or parent's anxiety rather than the child's. If this is the case, additional sessions for the parent or guardian who is experiencing the anxiety may be warranted.

Younger children's lack of cognitive understanding may protect them from the trauma, especially if no pain was involved in the abuse. Therefore, much of the work with a young child needs to involve the parent. The parent needs to learn to protect the child from unsupervised situations that are dangerous. The child needs to learn that what happened was "bad," a concept that a 3- or 4-year-old understands. A 3- or 4-year-old sexual abuse victim who is not acting out sexually and who no longer is exhibiting anxious behavior should be able to terminate therapy relatively quickly. Therapy should resume if the child begins acting out, and will most likely be necessary as she approaches adolescence and normal sexual urges and situations are activated. Older children seem to be more disturbed by sexual behavior than younger children, probably because of their increased understanding of sexual behavior. At latency and adolescence, aggressive and impulsive behaviors appear as reactions to abuse (Walker 1988).

Sexualized behavior is a response to abuse and a highly relevant treatment issue that is gaining much attention in research (Friedrich 1990, 1993a,b, Friedrich et al. 1991, 1992, Gil and Johnson 1993). When children take on sexualized roles that are seductive or sexually aggressive, this behavior by necessity becomes the major focus of treatment. The behavior must stop, because it sets the child up for repeated victimization, or begins setting a pattern for future perpetration. Sexualized play, which is the child's means of gaining a sense of control and mastery over what has happened, is often acted out inappropriately in a child's social interactions. The reasons for sexual acting out can be attributed to both behavioral and emotional responses to sexual abuse (Friedrich 1990). Because sexual activity can be a pleasurable experience, even in abusive situations, the behavior is apt to be repeated. Parents of children who have been sexually abused and who are exhibiting sexual behavior have to be reminded that we cannot take away the experience of awakened sexuality, but we can attempt to redirect and control it. In terms of object relations, there has been an internalization of sexual reactions in certain relationships; when a similar situation is presented, the child reacts according to the model that has been internalized (Friedrich 1990). Treatment of sexual abuse victims who are acting out requires a combination of setting up consequences for inappropriate sexual behavior as well as allowing for therapy to help the child channel and redirect these impulses. Consequences might be removing the child from the playroom when she engages other children in sexual activity, or having a child who is openly masturbating go to her room. If one completely takes away the ability for the child to act out sexually, one is stifling her ability to gain mastery and control over sexual impulses. Friedrich (1990) recommends that parents normalize masturbatory behavior by providing a place and a time when this behavior can occur. For a child who is already acting out the behaviors, the opportunity to act out sexual impulses with dolls and dollhouses, art materials, or anatomical dolls can be an appropriate means of rechanneling these impulses.

In the case of sexual abuse victims, therapy needs to be approached from two levels. First, the therapist must offer opportunities for symbolic enactment of abuse and the conflictual feelings that accompany it, both of which will encompass relationship issues. As has been stated, art and play therapy are natural modalities in which this can occur, as are other expressive therapies. Second, psychological education directly addressing issues of safety is imperative in order to help prevent the child from becoming a repeated victim or a perpetrator.

A further consideration when outlining treatment strategies is the child's history of placement if she is in foster care. Although she may have achieved psychological educational goals, the object relations issues become far more important for a child who has had numerous placements. It is not at all unusual for a child to have had eleven or twelve different placements in half as many years. The scenarios vary, but the following case is typical.

> Loretta, whose mother was a prostitute and drug addict, was removed from her home at age 3 because of abuse and neglect. She was placed in a foster home, but because of sexual acting-out behavior was removed and subsequently placed in three other foster homes before being transferred to a residential treatment facility. She did very well with the structure in the residential treatment center, and made behavioral gains, so at age 6 she was moved to a foster home. However, she could not bond with the foster parent and began acting out aggressively. Subsequently, she was moved to another foster home, where she continued to act out and was hospitalized to be evaluated for medication. After hospitalization, she was sent to another residential treatment facility, and thus a child who was not yet 8 had had nine different living situations.

The therapist may be the child's only constant object. When a child is being moved from home to home, having one consistent person in her life is an often overlooked beneficial product of treatment. A therapist who looks at the child's placement record and sees more than three or four placements needs to question the advisability of providing just one more short-term relationship. In situations where the child cannot bond, the crucial healing element will be the process of bonding with one person.

◖◎ 4 ◎◗

When Words Are Not There: The Preverbal Child, Ages 0 to 2

Therapy for preschoolers is limited in terms of what they can remember, what they can process cognitively, and how many preventive skills concepts they are capable of learning. However, because of their use of behavioral enactments, play, and scribble drawing accompanied by storytelling, they are able to make use of art and play therapy and can begin to work through issues on a symbolic level, independent of verbal processing.

Typically, children do not enter therapy before age 2 or 3, and sometimes much later. However, many children brought into treatment were actually traumatized much earlier, at preverbal stages. The chronological age of the child may be much higher than the level at which he is arrested emotionally, due to a history of severe deprivation and abuse. The art can be a clue to the child's emotional and cognitive functioning level (Levick 1989, Lowenfeld and Brittain 1987, Silver 1990). When a child enters therapy and is still in the scribble stage of art development, it suggests that the level of therapeutic intervention begin at a much earlier level than the child's chronological age may suggest. The examples presented in this chapter are typical of children who fall into this category. Their chronological age varies, but they share in common a functioning level at the sensorimotor stage (Piaget and Inhelder 1969), and at the scribble stage of art development (Lowenfeld and Brittain 1987).

> "This is Bad John," Suzie said as she drew a circle (see Figure 4–1). "He bad. He whoop me with a belt" (begins scribbling red). "He touch his dookie to my booty. He peed on me. He nasty. . . . He lick my coochie."
>
> Suzie, an extremely precocious and verbal 2½-year-old, came into therapy because of sexual abuse by her mother's boyfriend, substantiated by the existence of a venereal disease.

Figure 4–1. Two-year-old's picture of her perpetrator

At age 2½, she did not have elaborate cognitive processes available to her, despite her well-developed verbal skills. Suzie's primary presenting problem was sexual acting-out behavior. She initiated taking off clothes and fondling with other children in her preschool and in her neighborhood. It was imperative at this stage that the behavior cease, for her seductiveness included flirtations with any available men, and she was setting herself up for further victimization. She was capable of understanding the concepts of good and bad. Preventive skills focused on identification of the perpetrator as bad. Suzie would draw pictures of him and say "Bad John!" and then hit, smear, scribble, or spit on the picture. Suzie seemed more angry at the fact that he hit her with a belt than she was about the sexual abuse, which she may not have understood and which may not have been as painful as the beating. Therapy needed to focus on her mother as much as on Suzie. Mother needed to learn better supervision skills and how to initiate appropriate consequences for sexual acting-out behavior. Consequences included time-outs, removal of Suzie from contact with her friends when she engaged in this kind of play, and talking to Suzie about good and bad touch. As Suzie became more educated about good and bad touch, she spontaneously began disclosing more about the sexual abuse. Suzie's repeated pictures of Bad John and her defacing of them helped her gain mastery over her fear of him.

DEVELOPMENTAL ISSUES

The sensorimotor period, occurring during the first two years of life, is marked by parallel processes of a transition from undifferentiation to differentiation in both cognitive and affective life (Greenspan 1979). This can be seen in the child's first drawing attempts—which are, of course, scribbles. The first stage of scribbling is even termed the undifferentiated scribble. According to Lowenfeld and Brittain (1987), the child at this stage is merely making random marks with no attempt at organization or control. Color and placement are random, and the process is a kinesthetic experience that has no cognitive or symbolic meaning for the child. Children rapidly move into the stage of the controlled scribble, wherein they begin to repeat motions and watch the scribbles emerge while they are drawing. Placement is becoming more deliberate, although the child still does not have the inclination to draw objects, nor does he have the motor control necessary to do so. Children progress into the "named scribble stage" when they begin to relate marks to things they know, such as "me" or "mommy." This process usually begins with prompting from others and the child, to please the other, may assign a name to a scribble. This reflects an important developmental gain—an awareness of and desire to please another. It is an interactive response that gives the child pleasure. The identification of the subject may change in the process of drawing, as the child is not actually using symbolism at this point. The child at this stage will begin to form circles, and ultimately will combine shapes to make suns and primitive humanoids (Lowenfeld and Brittain 1987).

Through the child's art, even at this early stage, the therapist may identify intrusive phenomena and understand better what the trauma issues are for him (Nader and Pynoos 1991). The artwork may point toward particular areas of stress for him, as evidenced by such indicators as excessive scribbling, scribbling over, and other graphic indicators. A child as young as 2 can show signs of stress through the kinds of scribbles made (Lowenfeld and Brittain 1987).

During the sensorimotor period, children begin to develop concepts of space, time, and causality, a scheme of permanent objects, the ability to combine schemes, and the beginning of memory (Piaget and Inhelder 1969). All of these concepts will be continually refined as the child develops.

THE CHILD'S UNDERSTANDING OF TRAUMA

A child's ability to process trauma during this stage is limited. Terr (1985) suggest that before about age 28 months, a child does not possess the capacity to take in, retain, or retrieve full traumatic images in words. Memories may be stored in a non-verbal form that is relatively inaccessible to him; however, visual memory may be available. When the visual memory is evoked, the child may act out the behavior. Some of this experience may be organized in imagery that relates to other sense systems, such as olfactory or tactile, and some may be in terms of schemes or action patterns. The memory may be acted out, but is not available to the child consciously. It is not until the preoperational phase of cognition, and the preoedipal or oedipal phases in the psychoanalytic sense, that the child develops what Piaget calls the semiotic (symbolic) function (Piaget and Inhelder 1969), in which the capacity for memory appears. Greenspan (1979) states that the absence of memories from the earliest years of life is not a function of repression, but of the lack of cognitive structures in the sensorimotor period.

Because of this, it may be that even art and play are not yet useful to the child in therapy. The therapist may need to begin therapy at an even earlier developmental level than is possible through art and play. Because memory is stored in the body, movement may be the place to start in terms of therapeutic interaction.

> During my first session with Kyle, age 3, I felt an unbelievable and overwhelming sense of sadness. He did not spontaneously explore the art or the playroom, as most 3-year-olds do. He did not look at me. He did not speak or smile or cry or frown. Kyle had just been released from the hospital, where he had been treated for multiple fractures, malnourishment, and head blows. His body and face had scars from cuts inflicted on him by his caretakers, when they would throw knives at him for being bad. His leg was in a cast. He had permanent rope scars on his wrist. He had spent much of his life in a closet. I wondered, because of his total lack of interaction with me, whether he would be treatable in an outpatient setting.
>
> I asked Kyle if he wanted to touch the sand in the sandtray as he stood looking at it. He shook his head. I asked if he wanted to hold a doll. He shook his head. I asked if he wanted to sit on my lap. He nodded. I put him on my lap, and I softly told him that I would not hurt him, and that he could play with any of the toys that he saw. He did not squirm in my lap, as 3-year-olds do. He sat stiffly, too frightened to move even one part of his body, for a full thirty minutes.
>
> After our encounter, I spoke to the foster mother about his need for safety and nurturing, suggesting that she allow him to control all interactions at first. Although she had never had a foster child like this, her instincts were excellent. For

example, she reported that he hoarded food, and as an intervention she allowed him to save his last bite of food from meals in a zip-lock bag that he could carry with him. I hoped that he could bond with this foster mother, because our fifty-minutes-per-week together was too short a time to overcome a past of such early deprivation.

In our second session, Kyle began exploring the therapy room. Developmentally, Kyle could not take advantage of art therapy. His beginning scribbles were indicative of a child much younger, at the undifferentiated scribble stage, and scribbling did not hold his interest. He could not name his scribbles, so he was not yet able to use symbolism. He did not play as 3-year-olds typically do. Rather, he picked up toys and dropped them. He kinesthetically moved his hands through the sand but did not use toys to create movement or stories in it. Because he was in the earliest part of the scribble stage, reflecting developmental delays that suggested he was functioning at less than a 2-year-old level, Kyle's therapy had to begin at a much earlier stage of development than was possible through art and play. We began with movement. His foster mother, who had made a long-term commitment to his care, was brought in to sessions initially, to help in their bonding process and help him to feel more comfortable with me. Kyle responded to the Co-Oper Band™, a twelve-foot latex tube covered in brightly colored fabric, similar to a large rubber band. We encouraged interaction with the Band and gradually Kyle explored and expanded his world of touch. At first, he got inside the Band with one of us, and pulled away. This pulling away motion was repeated many times. The Band allows children the opportunity to experiment with closeness and distance, and at this point in time Kyle was not ready to be closer than three or four feet. The person inside the Band with him would follow as he pulled, maintaining the distance between them. This game evolved into Kyle pulling toward one of us who was outside the Band, while the one inside the Band with him provided some tension in it, so that he had to work at reaching the person. Once he discovered this game, Kyle was ready to hug and be hugged back, and this was indicative of the trust that had developed. Kyle also discovered that he could wind the Band around himself, and be tied up. This game echoed parts of his abuse. What seemed to be important to him was the fact that when he said, "Help! Save me! I'm all tied up!" one of us would untangle him. He also played like he was "swimming" on the floor, and when he screamed for help, one of us would pull him toward us, rescuing him.

TREATMENT ISSUES

At this age, some of the goals of play and art therapy are aimed at supporting parental efforts at setting limits for acting-out behavior by providing alternative outlets for the child, allowing him an opportunity to be expressive with creative stimuli, and providing a nurturing atmosphere where he can experiment with a wider repertoire of adaptive behavior.

As Kyle attached to his foster mother, he also became stimulated sexually, which is not uncommon in children sexually abused at very young ages. He attempted to come into the bathroom when she was showering, and when she emerged wearing a towel, he would become excited and begin hump-ing on her legs. He also became stimulated when she wore summer tops and shorts, and would attempt to unbutton her blouse, or French kiss her. All of these behaviors were extremely unsettling, and his foster mother asked for help in setting limits without making him feel bad or inadvertently teaching him that sex is dirty. Using his terminology, I told Kyle that I wanted to talk about "boyfriends and girlfriends." I provided anatomically correct dolls, and asked, "What do boyfriends and girlfriends do?" Kyle asked if he could undress the dolls. He pulled on the boy dolls' penises and stuck his fingers in the vaginas of the girl dolls. He positioned the dolls carefully, as if they were having sex. He said, "They kiss."

I told Kyle that when he and mommy play, they cannot play these games because mommies cannot do that with their little children. Mommies can only do that with daddies. He asked, "Then who can I do that with? You?" "No," I said. "You can do that with the dolls. When you feel excited like that, you can play with the dolls." In this way, I was putting words on his feelings for him (he gets "excited") and I was providing him a time and a place where he could do this kind of play, which seemed essential to his ability to ultimately control his sexual impulses. Together, we dressed the dolls. At the end of the session, we brought in his foster mother, and talked with her about what he and I discussed. I reminded Kyle that when he and mommy play, if he starts to feel excited, they have to stop playing. He cannot play like that with mommy or with other children. He can play with my dolls. I also reminded his foster mother that as soon as she notices his play becoming sexually charged, she needs to stop the play and remind him that they cannot play that game.

The child's language abilities at this stage are extremely limited. Because of the limitations of therapy for a child under the age of 2, most of the work will be done with the parents or guardians. The parent must take total responsibility for keeping the child safe, for at this age he is unable to identify or to learn about unsafe situations. The parent must learn to identify unsafe situations or people. The parent must also learn that a child of 2 who is sexually or aggressively acting out cannot be left alone unsupervised with other children.

The child's memory will not be aided by representations, symbols, or thoughts, but will be totally dependent upon perceptions and body movements. Therefore the abused child may use the body to recreate the abuse, and this behavior, when acted out in inappropriate settings, must be stopped in a gentle but firm manner. The parent will most likely be the one to witness this behavior, so educating the parent is paramount. For example, a 2-year-old who takes off her clothes repeatedly and puts objects in her vagina should consistently have the clothes put back on, and be given a firm "No!" The child should not be punished beyond this, for she is only repeating behavior that has been learned without understanding why. As the child develops language, the parent may talk to her about it, but the response of "No" must be consistently repeated.

Any therapy with the child will be primarily expressive in nature. A therapist trained in art and play therapy will want to offer the child opportunities for enactment through presentation of materials that invite repetition. Some of the toys, particularly the anatomically correct dolls, may appear to be stimulating to the child. However, they will not be sexually stimulating to a child who does not already have that issue (Dawson et al. 1992, Sivan et al. 1988). When a child appears to be sexually stimulated within the session, the therapist may want to steer the child toward the dolls, as it offers an opportunity for enactment in a safe way. Dolls, puppets, and in particular anatomically correct dolls, can stimulate the kind of play that is useful toward enactment of abusive situations (Klorer 1995). Through repetition, the child can experiment with new modes of behavior or different outcomes. The child should not be allowed to remove his clothes or act in a sexually provocative manner in the office, but should be given dolls for this purpose.

The therapist will want to provide art materials for expressive purposes. Although the child may be only scribbling, the stories that he tells about the scribbles may be meaningful, especially in the Named Scribble stage. Play and drawing tap into primary process thinking, which helps the therapist to understand the child's mental representations of the event. Play and art provide opportunities for the child to reexamine, find new meaning for, reexperience, and rework the memory and the emotions associated with the trauma, independently of verbal processing.

For a child living in a secure family environment with a strong parental support system, therapy at this stage of development may be short-term, with the understanding that he may need further therapy as he matures. However, one should not make the mistake of thinking that because the child has no verbal or conscious memory of abuse there has been no trauma. If the event is being symbolically reenacted in art or play, it suggests that there has in fact been severe trauma, and that he is using expressive means to gain mastery over the anxiety associated with the event. By providing an expressive outlet for this anxiety, the therapist is assisting him in working through the abuse. The need to process the abuse verbally, other than to learn new prevention skills, does not belong to the child.

> Carla, a 3-year-old, came into therapy because of suspicions of sexual abuse. The father, whom she visited on weekends, was named as the possible perpetrator. Carla had shown a number of behavioral clues that indicated there was much trauma, although she could not disclose the nature of that trauma in any detail. Her behavior at home included excessive scrubbing of her genital area with a plastic brush, demonstration of sexual positions in her play with dolls, masturbation, sudden phobic fear of hair in her mouth, a sudden reaction to the point of nausea to any white, sticky food, and nightmares in which Carla would wake up screaming. She was able to disclose only that her dad "hurt my butt" and that "Daddy and a mean lady put fire in my butt." Carla was a bright and precocious child, but could never offer enough details to substantiate a child abuse case with the state's protective services organization. In therapy, she appeared to be afraid to talk on some occasions, but on other occasions she appeared to dissociate. Always, daddy's name evoked anxiety for Carla. When I asked her about daddy, she would sometimes make weird movements with her head and then stare off into space, suggestive of dissociation, or she would lie down on the floor and began writhing, as her eyes rolled around in her head. Other times she might run out of the room in distress, or flit around from one activity to the next, seeming to illustrate the principle that you can't hit a moving target (Walker 1988). Carla would have been 2 years old at the time of the abuse, so her memories may have been

preverbal, and hence she would not have access to descriptive words to convey exactly what happened then. During the sensorimotor period, construction of mental structures is not aided by representations, symbols, or thoughts, but rather such schemes are totally dependent upon perceptions and body movements (Piaget and Inhelder 1969). Her avoidance and dissociative behavior whenever daddy's name was mentioned, and her vague admissions, along with sexual acting-out behavior, were such that sexual abuse with her father as perpetrator was highly suspected, and the immediate concern was to get legal intervention so that he would have no unsupervised visitation. Once this was accomplished, I felt that creating further trauma through "therapy" that attempted to get the child to remember and disclose details was not in Carla's best interest at this time, since she was safe from further abuse. Because several months had gone by since Carla had seen her father, and her mother and she had moved to a new area, very little from their previous life was available anymore to stimulate memories, so she was becoming even less verbal about the memories. Consequently, a more subdued and nondirective approach to therapy was used, with unstructured playtime and art-making available for her to choose and direct her own therapy.

Carla's play therapy themes indicated a number of fears, including fears of monsters, spiders, the dark, and bad people. Ultimately, through repetition of themes, Carla was able to gain more control of her anxieties. Toward the end of therapy, play therapy themes began to take on a more positive character, such as sandtray themes of mother animals taking care of their baby animals and living "happily ever after." Therapy was terminated when Carla turned 4. The decision to terminate was made when nightmares had ceased and Carla was generally observed to be less anxious and better able to cope with stressful situations. At that time, I recommended that further therapy would be warranted as Carla got older, almost inevitably at adolescence. For a period of time I became more directive, working with Carla on sexual abuse–prevention techniques through reading books about potentially abusive situations for animals and children, and having Carla repeat ways for the characters to stay safe. She also worked on identification of simple feelings (happy, sad, scared) through drawings.

Awareness of other people's feelings and the ability to identify specific situations that evoke different kinds of affective responses are important in learning prevention techniques. Although children are primarily egocentric, studies (Borke 1971, 1972, Greenspan 1979) suggest that children as young as 3 can differentiate between happy and unhappy feelings in other people. Games that allow the child an opportunity to learn simple feelings will complement the treatment.

We can hope that children under age 2 or 3 will tend to forget their traumas. Terr (1985) suggests that some do so because of the massive repressions normal in the first years of life, and some because the trauma occurred at a time when the child had not yet acquired adequate words or symbols to represent and record the trauma. This has vast implications for the therapist working with children under the age of 3. It justifies the use of art and play therapy as the primary therapy, and poses the question of whether it is even appropriate for the therapist to get children to talk about the abuse, for fear of leading them in a direction about which they are not able to process cognitively. Terr (1990) suggests that before about age

28 months, a child does not possess the mental capacity to take in, retain, or retrieve full traumatic images in words. Yet behavioral memory manifested in play is almost universal.

In terms of memory, a child is more likely to remember a single traumatic episode than repeated trauma. This is because in a singular event the child does not have the foresight to activate defenses that would help him cope with the fear. Events that occur over time, however, stimulate defenses such as denial, splitting, self-anesthesia, and dissociation (Terr 1990). Certainly in Carla's case, dissociation appeared to be activated as a defense. Her abuse was suspected to have been repeated over a number of months and hence she was able to anticipate its occurrence with her visits to her father. She learned to activate her defensive coping strategies in order to tolerate her fear and she showed evidence of being severely distressed and disturbed. Always, we need to remember that the defenses the child has employed have served him well.

Nurturance often becomes a primary issue in therapy for children of this age, and the therapist may also need to educate the parent about how to nurture the child. Parents who were not nurtured themselves may not know how important this is. The therapist may need to take an active nurturing role with the child himself, including hugging, rocking, and holding. For children with sexual abuse histories, touch is a very sensitive issue. The therapist should be open to touch, but should allow the child to control when and how touch happens. Because of the interactive nature of art and play therapy, the therapist can test out the child's receptivity to touch through the exchange of art materials or dolls. For very young children, the therapist might walk with his or her hand to the side and see if the child grasps it. Insecure children tend to reach for it eagerly. In time, the child may initiate lap sitting or snuggling. The therapist should be aware that a child of this age is likely to confuse sexuality and nurturing, and be ever on the lookout for moments when this confusion is occurring in order to help the child to understand his sexual feelings.

> I walked into the waiting room to meet my new client, a 3-year-old who been placed in a foster home only two weeks earlier. Renita ran toward me and hugged my legs as I entered the room. She was tiny for her age, and could only hug as high as my knees. I turned to her social worker and asked if Renita always greeted strangers in this manner. He did not know.
>
> Inside my office, Renita and I sat at the art table. Renita asked where I lived. I reflected the question back to her. "Nowhere," she answered. She said she used to live with her real mom, and did not know why she doesn't live there anymore. As we were talking, she scribbled with markers on the paper available. She could not name her scribbles, as a typical 3-year-old would be able to, and did not know her colors. She filled the paper with heavy-pressured lines and dots. After drawing, she explored the rest of the room with me, and discovered the dollhouse, sandtray, puppets, and dolls. She moved quickly from toy to toy, not seeming to enjoy the play, but wanting to cover as much territory as possible.
>
> When there were five minutes remaining in the session, we put away the toys she used and I gave her a sticker. She ran to the sticker drawer and began taking things out of the drawer. I told her she could not do this, and told her it was time to go, but that I would like to see her next week. Renita got very clingy and sad, and big tears flowed down her tiny

face. She climbed up onto my lap and cried. By this time, I had another client waiting. I reassured her that I would see her again, and walked her out to the waiting room. As soon as I let go of her hand, she ran back into my office. I went to get her, but this time I carried her out, and handed her to the waiting arms of her social worker.

There was little information about Renita's history. When a child this young comes into foster care, it is often because of extreme neglect. The details and extent of abuse come much later, in bits and pieces, through the child's behavior, play, and words.

Renita began to form a more genuine attachment to me in the ensuing weeks. The first play ritual that she established was with the Co-Oper Band. Renita was in control of the Band. When we got inside of it together, she pulled away and came toward me only a few feet before pulling back again. Each time she'd come toward me, she said in a sing-songy voice, "I want YOU!" but then would pull back before she got too close. Then she began wrapping herself up in the Band, twirling toward me and getting all tangled, while saying, "I want you, I want you, I want you, I want you, I want YOU!" At this point she would be all tangled up very close to me. Possibly because of the closeness this game allowed, this ritual led to playing "Baby." Of course, Renita assigned herself to the role of the baby, and I was the mommy. I had to be clear with the boundaries of this game, as I did not want Renita to begin regressing at home or in her daycare, so I was careful to define the parameters of the play area, and when we moved back to the art area I always reminded her that she was no longer a baby, but was big girl Renita again. She was able to differentiate between the game and reality.

The first time she played "Baby," Renita enacted the movements of an 8-month-old baby who has just mastered crawling toward things and reaching for what she wants. Her enactments were an almost perfect replication. Children often reenact an age at which their basic needs were not sufficiently met. They seem to know instinctively what it is that they missed and need. She crawled toward "mommy" and I reached out my arms toward her. She reached for the bottle and I fed her. She cuddled close to me and I rocked her. Renita always controlled the amount of touching that happened, and she seemed to crave the physical contact. Renita did not tire of this game easily. She was ensuring that her unmet nurturance needs were satisfied. After several weeks of "Baby," Renita's baby movements became more like a 1½-year-old. She pulled herself up as if she were beginning to learn to walk. Her movements were strikingly realistic. In this phase, she explored more autonomously away from "mommy." She would crawl behind the dollhouse, and play "Where's baby?" through the windows. She played "peek-a-boo." She would walk toward the sandtray toys, speaking baby talk, and pick up toys that looked interesting, as if she were discovering them for the first time.

After about five months of working together, Renita came into her session and immediately wanted to play "Baby" again. She sat on my lap with the bottle and cuddled close to me. She whined, "I want my mommy," so I fed her and held her. She wanted to be very close. Suddenly, she got up off my lap and said in her regular voice, "Now I a little kid.

I'm 3." The 3-year-old stirred the sand and pretended to make popsicles for her and her mommy.

After several minutes of being 3, she announced, "Now I going to be the daddy." The daddy made food in the sandtray, fed the baby doll, and put the baby doll to bed. The daddy, mommy, and doll went on a car trip. When we returned, he gave the baby a bath, brushed her teeth, and put her to bed. "Now we go to bed," Renita announced. I lay back on the pillow I was sitting on, and Renita lay next to me. "Go to sleep!" Renita demanded. I pretended to be asleep. Suddenly, Renita started to get sexually stimulated. She kissed me quickly on the lips, began breathing heavier, and ran her fingers softly along my neck and shoulder, all in a matter of seconds. I was startled, sat up immediately, and told Renita that we could not play that game. I told her adults cannot play that game with children. Renita looked confused and hurt. I told her that when she wants to play that game, she can use my anatomical dolls. I asked if she wanted them and she said yes. Renita took the dolls and said, "Him going to hump her." She began with the adult male and female dolls, undid the man's pants and said, "Him put his dick in her and hump her." She very carefully put the male doll's penis into the female's vagina and began pushing on his buttocks rhythmically with her hand. She then repeated this with the child dolls.

After we put the dolls away and moved back to the art table, I sat down and said I wanted to tell her something. Again I told her that adults and children cannot play that game. We can play "Baby," and I can hold her and feed her, but we cannot play adult games. Renita looked very sad and rejected. In future sessions, I was more aware of the potential for her to misperceive situations and set firmer boundaries on our play. Renita learned that when she feels that kind of excitement she can use the dolls to play.

This was a highly sexualized child who likely received affectionate touches only during abuse. I needed to help her understand the feelings that were activated in her body so that she could begin to differentiate the two. Her confusion of nurturing and sexuality was understandable, and quite complex for a child of this age to understand. I talked at length to her foster mother about her own interactions with Renita, as I correctly assumed that if it happened in my office it was happening elsewhere. I made suggestions as to how to set limits when Renita appeared to be confused. I suggested that she allow Renita to touch her own genitals when alone in her bed, but not at other times. When goodnight kisses took on a sexual nuance, I suggested the foster mother tell Renita that mothers and daughters do not kiss like that.

When working with a child of a very young age, or an older child who is functioning emotionally at a regressed stage of development because of past deprivation and abuse, one immediately needs to assess the possibility of working with the parents or guardians to help them learn to deal with behaviors as they arise. Because the parents will be most likely to witness the acting-out behavior, it is almost impossible to have an effect on behavior without their help. Working with the parent to find a consistent reaction to behavior will help the child learn on a cognitive level what is appropriate and inappropriate. This then coincides with the therapist's expressive work with him, wherein we attempt to help him understand the feelings that accompany the behavior. This is accomplished through following his lead in terms of choices of materials and types of interaction, such as movement, art, and play. The therapist will need to put words on feelings for the child of this age as they are being expressed, remembering, however, that the need to process verbally does not belong to the child. As the child matures, he will be able to make more use of symbolism in art and play.

«© 5 ©»

"Mommy Hates Me 'Cause I'm Bad": The Early School-Aged Child, Ages 2 to 7

"Some boys hurt my behind. It was big boys and little boys. First they said they were going to marry me. And then they killed me in the behind. They put ice on it 'cause they didn't want me to tell my mom. And they killed me and they shot me in the behind and they licked my behind." This memory came to 5-year-old Vickie as she played with the anatomical dolls.

When Vickie was 2, her mother went to the store one day, leaving Vickie and her three sisters alone. She never returned. Vickie was placed with an aunt for about a year, and was removed from that home when it was discovered that she was being beaten. She was then placed in a foster home. This foster mother had an extremely negative perception of Vickie and insisted that the child needed to be institutionalized. Vickie was referred to therapy to assess the situation. Her first picture eloquently revealed her feelings about the foster mother. She drew herself standing in the rain. When asked to tell a story about her picture, Vickie said, "It started to rain on the grass and my [foster] mother didn't bring me no coat and it started to rain and there was nowhere for me to go." Vickie struggled with maternal rejection issues, and confused her mother's actions with actions of the foster mother. "My foster mom hates me—she does hate me for real. It know it 'cause Jesus told me. Jesus likes me. Jesus told me my mommy hates me. She hates me. My mommy hates me for real. I know 'cause she hits me and swings me around. . . . She spanks me when I don't do nothing. I'm talking about my foster mom. No, I'm talking about my mommy." Vickie was confused because Jesus talked to her, and other voices in her head told her to like the Devil and to do bad things. The week therapy began, her foster mother requested Vickie's removal, purportedly because of her behavior, and the foster parent immediately got a new foster child who went to Vickie's school. This contributed to Vickie's internalized self-image as being an unwanted and unlovable child. She projected this onto her new preadoptive foster mother, and said, "My new mommy is ugly—that's what the voices in my brain said. I don't like it when they say that. The voices make me mad. They say 'stupid' and 'ugly' and they say the Devil is right. They say the Devil is their boyfriend. I don't like that. They say they like the Devil. They tell me not to like my new mommy."

Vickie's foster mother offered her something new: love, consistency, and firm boundaries. Slowly, Vickie began to trust and then bond with her. Vickie continued in therapy for two years, until her adoption was complete. At termination of treatment she was no longer exhibiting any behavior problems and was doing exceptionally well in school, dancing classes, and soccer.

At Vickie's age, hearing voices is not necessarily a sign of psychosis. Magical thinking is normal. In fact, she stopped hearing voices shortly after she went to her pre-adoptive foster home, which was a much more loving environment that offered her the security she desperately needed.

Vickie's understanding of her abuse was typical for her age. Her memories were clear and her words reflected a 5-year-old's understanding of sexual abuse. She could verbalize what happened, although she did not know who the boys were. Her feelings about the abuse were accessible to her; this incident made her feel angry. Working with children at this stage of development opens up new possibilities for treatment because of their capacity for memory, their use of symbolism, and their ability to use art and play in more expressive ways.

DEVELOPMENTAL ISSUES

The preoperational period, extending from approximately 2 to 7 years of age, is marked by a movement toward representation of the world through signs and symbols (Piaget and Inhelder 1969). The child's ability to imitate and represent on a symbolic level may be independent of verbalization or conscious thought. For her, play becomes a primary means of expression. Because play is a natural progression of development that is at its height during this period, it is most useful to stay in her play metaphors in therapy, rather than trying to bring the issues to conscious awareness or verbalization. Consequently, I did not interpret for Vickie, although I would try to put words on her feelings for her.

> Within the first few weeks of therapy, Vickie developed a game of being a baby. The first time she did this, she crawled around the room as if exploring it for the first time. Vickie's movements were true to a baby of about 8 months of age. She also repeated early infant movement patterns, such as sucking, touching my cheek with her hand, and lying in a fetal position with a bottle. This use of symbolism eloquently allowed her to imitate and re-create earlier experiences. She became cuddly at this stage of her therapy, using scooting and pulling motions to come toward me and move away from me, as if still in the practicing subphases of the symbiotic attachment. She would pull herself toward me, and mouth my cheek rather than biting or kissing it. It seemed to be a sensual, not sexual, experience for her, as if she were discovering the world, and learning to trust, for the first time.

The beginning of this stage is marked by the development of the semiotic function, which includes language and thought development, a capacity for memory, and the ability to move between past and present. It contains the beginnings of mental representation, in which the child becomes capable of evocative memory, the ability to construct a mental image of a remembered object in the absence of that object (Greenspan 1979). Vickie remembered her mother. This ability to move between past and present helped her to understand her current feelings of sadness.

"I want to talk about my mom. She didn't say goodbye when she left me. She didn't give anybody her phone number. I remember her, but I don't know if she remembers me."

Part of the process of adoption was to help Vickie accept the fact that her mother would never come to get her. Like many children her age, Vickie's memories were selective, and she did not want to see her mother as bad or wrong.

"I remember her name," Vickie said one day when we were talking about her mother.

I said, "Your mom must have some problems."

Vickie started to cry and said, "My mom doesn't have problems. Don't say anything about my mom."

I said, "The reason you are going to get adopted is because your mom couldn't take care of you. Usually that means the mom has a problem. You are such a good girl and a cute girl so it *must* be because your mom has a problem; otherwise she would be able to take care of you."

Vickie put her hands on her ears. She did not want to hear this.

As Vickie's therapy progressed, she did remember more details about her past. She recalled siblings. She said she lived with her mother longer than the other children did. "'Cause they were grown up. Seven years or older and you gots to leave. But me, I got to stay 'cause I was still little. They were lazy kids and that's why they had to leave." She said that she cried whenever she heard slow songs, suggesting that memories were evoked by auditory stimuli. She cried whenever she heard a song by Michael Jackson with the words, "You are not alone. I am here with you . . ."

Her continued use of symbolism helped her to play act her feelings of not being protected, but also allowed her to create more positive outcomes. For a period of time, we played that the ceiling lights were firebombs trying to get us. We had to keep running around my office to escape them. This game evolved into building a "safe house" from pillows and beanbag chairs so that the firebombs could not get us. We cuddled in the safe house.

In terms of a child's art development, the semiotic function coincides with the beginnings of figurative drawing, first in the form of circles with radials extending out, which develop into crude humanoids and later develop into figures that represent people in the child's life. The child's art is reflective of her egocentricity, and figures float in space. The child moves from the early figurative stage into the pre-schematic stage during this time period. Art becomes a means of communication with the self and another. The child determines the placement, size, and color of objects in a subjective manner. Color is used emotionally rather than representationally, and distortions and omissions are to be expected. She is searching for ways to depict her world, and is searching for a schema in which to represent it (Lowenfeld & Brittain 1987).

At the preoperational stage, art and play therapy are extremely useful modalities in therapy. Anthropomorphic qualities are attributed to inanimate objects, and the boundary between fantasy and reality is blurred (Greenspan 1979). Magical thinking can be pronounced at this stage, and the child's natural symbolic language and capacity for imagination can reveal much about her fears and anxieties. In Vickie's case, magical thinking is intertwined in her thought development. The Devil represents bad, and Jesus is good, and Vickie struggles to figure out the nature of her current relationships in connection to her past.

THE CHILD'S UNDERSTANDING OF TRAUMA

With the beginnings of language and thought development comes a capacity for remembrance of trauma, both with words and through evocative memory and the ability to construct a mental image of the trauma. Memory can be represented through signs and symbols. This stage marks the ability to move between past and present.

Children's concept of causality is poorly differentiated (Greenspan 1979). They may believe that bad things happen to them because they are bad. This logical conclusion can also tie in with their splitting mechanisms, as described earlier in Chapter 3. In terms of trauma related to abuse, children may begin to take on responsibility for the abuse, believing it happened because they deserved it.

> Donny, aged 3, was living in a foster home because of physical and sexual abuse perpetrated by his mother and stepfather. Donny's mother was extremely inconsistent in her visitation, and Donny's behavior in his foster home regressed drastically each time a visit was scheduled. He had done $1,500 worth of damage to his foster home the last time she did not visit, and was in danger of losing his placement in the home if this behavior continued. I asked Donny why his mother did not visit him as had been planned. Donny answered, "Because I was bad." This suggests both the psychological reaction of internalizing the bad object as well as

the cognitive function of his present age. He did not understand the nuances of causality and based his conclusion on
something that was logical to him. He *had* been bad, although his badness occurred after the event, not before. I
explained that his social worker told me mother did not visit
because she went shopping instead. Then I asked again why
his mother did not visit. "Because I was bad." After several
repeated explanations, Donny was able to say, "Because she
went shopping." However, he still could not put his own
feeling into this action until his foster father said, "That
makes me mad when she does that." This comment had the
effect of giving Donny permission to feel mad. Donny's play
for the rest of the hour consisted of knocking down the
mother doll in the sandtray and saying that his mom hurt
his feelings and he was mad. Two weeks later, his mother
failed to show up for family therapy. In individual therapy,
I asked Donny why she did not come and he said, "Because
I was bad." As difficult as it is to confront the child with the
truth of a parent's rejection, it is important that the therapist not let the child distort and take on responsibility for
parental failures, particularly at this age.

As the child matures in the preoperational stage, secondary process thinking evolves. The child begins to understand
means–ends relationships at the level of internal representations. Greenspan (1979) suggests that in psychological representations, the child can now discriminate between those
events based solely on his or her internal experiences and those
based on his or her external experiences. The child has the
ability, at the psychological level, to differentiate self from non-
self. In abuse cases, the child can more clearly differentiate

between the self and the perpetrator, and can assign different feelings to both individuals.

The child's capacity for memory is enhanced at this stage. Initially, however, memory is limited to reproductive images, or sights that have been perceived previously. Reproductive images can include static configurations, movements, and transformations, although static configurations are the most common until age 7 or 8 (Piaget and Inhelder 1969). An example of a static configuration is seen in the drawing made by a 6-year-old girl who was sexually abused. After reading a story with a theme of "this is my body," she spontaneously repeated the theme in her drawing (see Figure 5–1). It reads, "This is my body and it belongs to me." The child is not able to take in any more than what was presented in the book, but through repetition she is learning about her body and its private parts.

Figure 5–1. Six-year-old's picture: "This is my body and it belongs to me."

TREATMENT ISSUES

Some basic goals of therapy at this stage are to help the child learn to recognize and discriminate between feelings and offer opportunity for the expression of feelings in multi-expressive modalities; encourage exploration of her internalization of self as a bad object; and provide a nurturing environment where she can experiment with a wider range of adaptive behavior. At this stage, the ability to attach or form a therapeutic relationship with the therapist is crucial to any work being accomplished. For abused children, an additional goal is to teach the child basic rules of safety and abuse-prevention skills. Other therapeutic goals, particularly related to behavior, should be individualized for the particular child in treatment.

Treatment issues that are particularly relevant for abused children involve the child's internalization of guilt, shame, and sadness. The self as a bad object will be a long-term issue that is introduced at this stage. Because at this stage the boundary between fantasy and reality is blurred, the child feels that what happened was her fault. However, she also has the ability, at the psychological level, to differentiate self from non-self. Separating out feelings about the perpetrator and the self is a key treatment issue.

In terms of therapy, psychological education aimed at teaching the child new responses is appropriate at this stage. Through repeating or copying images, the child can learn how to respond to abusive situations. It is a good time to read books to children about sexual abuse so that they can learn new responses. For example, after being read a book about touching problems, a 7-year-old girl spontaneously drew Figure 5–2. She said, "This is a happy face, a sad face, a dollar to buy things

Figure 5–2. Seven-year-old girl's picture drawn after hearing a story about sexual abuse

with, and a book. The book is about a girl and somebody touched her privates and she ran away. She ran home. Her mom was home and she told her mom about it. Her mom said, 'That man cannot do that anymore.'" The scenario she depicted was very similar to the story read. The child's means of processing at this stage was through repetition of the story.

The primary issues in psychological education at this stage are ones of safety. Children should be able to identify kinds of good touch and kinds of bad touch. Children should be able to identify who they can go to and tell if they feel unsafe. Children should be able to repeat simple safety rules.

Because so many of the safety rules require the child to be able to discriminate between feelings (Liang et al. 1993)—both her own and someone else's—much work needs to be done in the area of identification of simple feelings. Children at this stage should be able to identify "happy," "mad," "scared," and "sad." Children should be able to play act and make faces corresponding with these feelings and identify them through pictures. Drawing pictures can aid in the process of learning to identify feelings.

Five-year-old Elinore's four pictures of feelings are typical of a child of this age and show how communication through art is possible (see Figures 5–3 through 5–6).

Despite Elinore's limitations in art, there are distinct differences between her depictions of happy, sad, mad, and scared. Notice how descriptive she is in her use of encapsulation for the figures that represent sad and scared, which suggests isolation or possibly a need for protection. Despite her

Figure 5–3. Five-year-old Elinore's picture of "happy"

Figure 5–4. Five-year-old Elinore's picture of "sad"

limited drawing skills, her artwork is reflective of her emotional world and egocentricity.

For children who have been severely abused, numbing of all feelings can be used as a defense, so it cannot be assumed that the child can discriminate between even simple feelings.

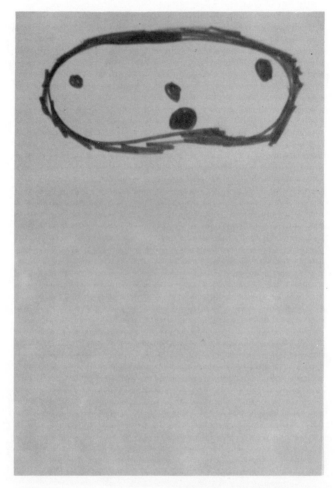

**Figure 5–5. Five-year-old Elinore's picture
of "scared"**

Figure 5–7 is by a 4-year-old who is just beginning to develop a schema for feelings and faces. Often, children of this age mix up feelings like scared and sad; however, this child demonstrates a good understanding that coincides with her ability to play act effective faces that show these feelings.

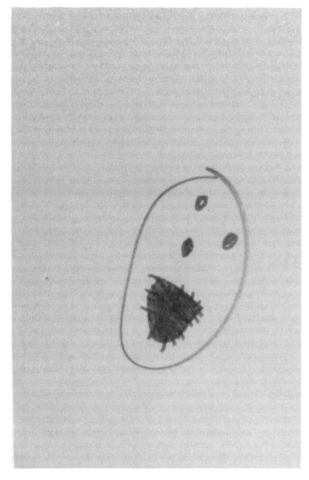

**Figure 5–6. Five-year-old Elinore's picture
of "mad"**

One way to help children learn to recognize and discriminate between feelings is to offer opportunity for the expression
of feelings in multi-expressive modalities. Dollhouses, dolls,
toy props, and other stimuli may provide the impetus the child
needs.

Figure 5–7. Four-year-old's "feelings"

DeMarcus was a 5-year-old boy whose abuse by an uncle included burning his feet in scalding water, head blows, and burns to his chest inflicted by a curling iron. DeMarcus's play and art themes were consistently violent. He perceived his world as unsafe and chaotic. Repeated themes of tornadoes eating up people, monsters that bite, snakes that chase people, and physical battles between adults and children were typical for DeMarcus. DeMarcus played in the dollhouse. "This is a story about a man and a boy. The man gets up and gets dressed and asks the boy if he ate yet. He told the boy to sit on a chair and then the man laid on the couch to sleep. The boy got up and picked up the sink and threw it on the man. Then he went upstairs and threw the refrigerator on the man. Then the man and the boy went on the roof and the boy threw the man off the roof and he died." Although themes of such violence are always a concern, the strength in DeMarcus was that he appeared to be containing this aggression within his play. His violent stories were balanced and tempered by delightful stories that included much detail and humor. There was no sign of him acting out aggressively at home or at school. He had a good support system and felt relatively safe now that his perpetrator was in jail. His mother and DeMarcus had a strong bond that obviously made him feel secure within himself. Therapy could be relatively short, because he appeared to be gaining mastery over his feelings of powerlessness through play, and was not acting out in his environment.

For the sexually acting-out child, the parent or guardian must be involved in the therapy. At this age, as in the sensorimotor stage of development, children must be given consequences for sexual acting-out behavior. The consequences are not punishments, but relate directly to the acting out and are designed to help them stop the behavior. The adult caretaker who observes the behavior must be very clear to the child that she cannot do these things and that she will be removed from the play situation every time the behavior occurs. If the child needs constant supervision, the caretakers must be willing to provide it.

Simultaneously, the therapist can talk to the child about the sexual behavior and provide opportunities for appropriate enactments within the safety of the office.

❦ 6 ❧

Feeling "Horrible, Stupid, Worried, Abused, Scared, Ugly": The Middle Years, Ages 7 to 12

Demetrius, a 9-year-old boy, drew hundreds upon hundreds of variations of what he termed "bottomless pits," in which a small person was falling. To make these, he usually used black crayon, marker, or pencil and began drawing on the edges of paper, spiraling inward toward the center. Inside the resulting hole in the center, Demetrius would draw a small person. Demetrius said that the person would never hit the bottom, but would continue to fall forever.

His houseparents, concerned about his compulsive need to repeat this image, brought me stacks of these drawings that they found lying around the house. Obviously, Demetrius had never been in one of these bottomless pits, but the feelings of helplessness, hopelessness, and despair seemed to be the key in the repetition and coincided with his abusive past. In art therapy, he drew more elaborate renditions following the same theme. He also drew intensely aggressive battles and wars, almost always choosing pencil because of the control it offered him (see Figure 6–1). Demetrius's behavior did not match his drawings. Behaviorally, he was an angelic child. I trust the art more than the behavior, however, and so considered him to be more disturbed than his twin brother, who acted out his anger in violent outbursts. Demetrius held his anger inside, but the art told the story of what was raging within. I found myself feeling hopeless and helpless at the end of sessions, as his drawings never had any resolution; people fell and never hit bottom, battles raged on with no ending.

Rarely in art or play do children enact in a factual way exactly what the trauma was that they experienced. Rather, the feelings evoked by the trauma are symbolically represented.

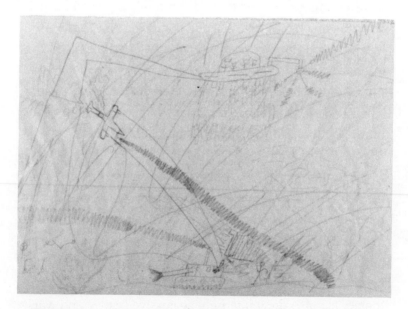

Figure 6–1. Nine-year-old boy's picture of a battle

The metaphors contained in the art are clues to the feelings the child is containing. With the cognitive and art-making abilities that with maturity come into the stage of concrete operations, the child has more opportunity to resolve traumatic issues on a metaphoric level.

DEVELOPMENTAL ISSUES

This stage of development begins at approximately age 6 or 7 and continues for another five years or more. The child has organized schemes within which he can simultaneously and almost automatically see the relationships between sets of variables (Greenspan 1979). This is seen in his artwork, for when he moves into the Schematic Stage of art development (ages 7 through 9), the artwork is marked by the repetition of schema. Up until this point, he has been searching for a concept to represent the world. Now, having found what he thinks it is, he has a need to repeat it (Lowenfeld and Brittain 1987).

The child begins to see the relationships between sets of variables and begins to understand concepts of space as being related to objects that are separated or in proximity to one another. In art, this means that figures no longer float in space, but are located through the appearance of an actual ground line on the picture plane. The child can understand the notion of the passage of time based on seriation of events, and inclusion of intervals between events occurring at certain points in time. Space–time representations can be seen in the artwork. The child can depict several events happening simultaneously, through the use of such graphic tricks as "x-ray vision," and can demonstrate the passage of time through sequential pictures (Lowenfeld and Brittain 1987).

As the child moves through the cognitive stage of concrete operations, he also progresses through stages in art making, moving from the Schematic Stage to the Stage of Dawning Realism, or the Gang Age, which occurs during latency, from approximately age 9 to 12. Rigid and more formal artwork evolves. Although the child gains in a capacity for detail, spontaneity is often lost and he frequently relies upon stereotypic artwork rather than venturing into untried territory. His artwork reflects a gradual abandonment of the reliable schema and a greater awareness of details. Less exaggeration, less distortion, and fewer omissions are evident. The child is much more aware of the environment, the picture plane with horizon line emerges in place of the base line, and he has a more complex view of the interrelationship between objects, using overlapping and size differences to convey a more realistic relationship between objects (Lowenfeld and Brittain 1987).

The child also gains in the capacity for figurative thinking. He begins to understand the concept of reciprocal relationships and reversibility (Greenspan 1979). The child at the operational stage experiences more stable self- and object representations through the ego's increasing capacity to deal with wishes, affects, and fears without the utilization of splitting (Greenspan 1979). In therapy it is a good time to help him process affective relationships by exploring more complex feelings, as he is able to understand nuances and subtle gradations between feelings, and can generalize and discriminate between certain feelings. This coincides, in art making, with a greater awareness of color and a move from rigid color–object relationships to more awareness of color differences and the nuances between different shades of the same color.

THE CHILD'S UNDERSTANDING OF TRAUMA

At this stage of development, the child can tolerate more stress and ambiguity than he once could, and he can integrate good and bad into one concept. Having achieved libidinal object constancy, he no longer needs to use splitting as a coping mechanism for dealing with negative feelings. This means he can explore feeling two different ways at the same time, which is a tremendous gain for the therapeutic process. In abuse cases, the child can now accept the concept of loving or liking certain things about the perpetrator, but hating the abuse. He is capable of integrating all feelings associated with the per-petrator into one multifaceted concept.

The defenses that develop at this stage are useful for the child and help him to tolerate the increasing ambiguities of life; these include reaction formation, rationalization, iden-tification, and further development of empathy (Greenspan 1979).

Although the child is cognitively capable of memory, the latency-age child tends to repress frightening feelings. Repres-sion is a normal part of development, and should be accepted by the therapist as normal. For the latency-age child who is becoming self-conscious and aware of his body in relation to others, insecurity abounds and awkwardness is the rule. Con-sequently, it is scarcely the time to expect him to directly ap-proach that which, in his eyes, makes him feel different. Therefore, we see the issues of abuse and trauma symboli-cally expressed in the art, not directly. The therapist should stay at the symbolic level with the child as long as the child needs to, making therapy a safe haven. The child will let the therapist know when he is ready to deal more directly with the issues, after trust has been firmly established.

In terms of the child's sexual development, Blos (1962) states that the idea that sexuality is latent during this period has been superseded by an acknowledgment of clinical evidence that sexual feelings—expressed in masturbatory, voyeuristic, exhibitionistic, and sadomasochistic activities—do not cease to exist during the latency period. Sexual activity during the latency period "serves as a regulator of tension, but this function is superseded by the emergence of a variety of ego activities, sublimatory, adaptive, and defensive in nature" (p. 54). For sexually abused children, sexual activity as a reaction to past abuse may persist throughout latency.

TREATMENT ISSUES

Some basic goals of therapy during this stage are to (1) form a therapeutic relationship with the child based upon safety and trust; (2) provide both verbal and nonverbal opportunities for expression of complex feelings, thus helping him learn to discriminate between gradations of feelings; and (3) help the child to experience feelings of empowerment through drama, art, play, movement, and other expressive means. For abused children, additional goals are exploring feelings about an abusive past using expressive modalities, working toward sublimation of aggressive or sexual impulses, and helping the child formulate his own basic rules of safety and sexual-abuse prevention skills. Other therapy goals will need to be individualized for each child in treatment.

At about age 7 or 8, the child's ability to move between past and present and to make anticipatory images allows him to begin to work on issues through the therapist's presentation of hypothetical situations. No longer does he need to rely on repetition of what has been taught, but rather he is now capable of actually creating a solution to a set problem.

> Demetrius continued to draw bottomless pits, almost reveling in the story of the person falling forever. Realizing that Demetrius's repetition was not helping him and that in fact he appeared to be stuck, I took a more active role in his stories. In one particular variation on this theme, Demetrius drew a story about a man in an airplane (see Figure 6–2). The plane exploded, and the man had no parachute, so he was falling. Normally, this would be the end of his picture, and the end of the story. "Demetrius, what would happen if the story continued, and didn't end here? I wonder what might happen next?" I asked. Demetrius then drew a volcano, and said the man was going to fall into the volcano, which was a bottomless pit. Feeling more hopeless, I suggested he think about what else might happen. With coaxing, Demetrius decided the man could fall into a soft snowbank instead, where he might freeze to death. I wondered aloud again what might happen next. Finally, Demetrius drew a small Indian village at the base of the mountain. An Indian hunter found the man, arranged for a rescue party, and took the man to his new home (see Figure 6–3).
>
> What was important in this interaction was that I merely suggested to Demetrius the possibility of a new ending, which he could accept or reject. The fact that he was able to work with it indicates that he was ready to do so, but he needed my assistance in knowing how to get there. By staying in the child's metaphor, but encouraging him to devise

**Figure 6–2. Nine-year-old boy's picture of
a man falling from an airplane**

a satisfactory ending to this story, I was helping him to find
the curative path in his repetition.

As stated earlier, for sexually abused children, sexual activity may persist throughout latency, although some children
may be capable of formulating sublimatory activities. The child
will continue to need consequences for sexual behavior, and
the consequences need to be age appropriate as the child gets

Figure 6–3. Nine-year-old boy's rescue theme

older and understands more about why the behavior is unacceptable. For example, whereas earlier the consequence was only to remove a child temporarily from a situation, a child of this age is making more conscious choices about behavior. Therefore, the parent needs to up the ante in terms of consequences. An appropriate consequence might be that he cannot do sleepovers, a popular activity for children of this age. If the child is known to act out sexually in some more innocuous situations, he certainly cannot be trusted to do any sleepovers! This rationale can be explained to the child. He needs to be given a strong message that this behavior is not acceptable. There can be no exceptions to the consequence until the behavior is known to have ceased.

SUBLIMATION

Sublimation is one of the healing qualities inherent in the expressive arts, and is something children at this stage employ as a natural course of development. This is exemplified in the case of 10-year-old Alicia (Klorer 1995).

> Alicia was a highly sexualized child, as can be seen in the "family portrait" that she spontaneously painted in a group art therapy session (see Figure 6–4). Alicia's sexual acting-out behavior was considered serious when her teachers began reporting frequent masturbation in school. At latency, masturbation is a typical means of sexual expression, but certainly discretion should already have been learned. Attempts to control this behavior through talking with Alicia were unsuccessful. Children in her class were beginning to ostracize her as a "nasty" girl, but this, too, had no apparent effect on the behavior, which seemed to increase with her classmates' derogatory comments.
>
> Alicia was introduced to the anatomically correct dolls in her therapy for sexual abuse. She almost always chose to play with the dolls during her session, seemingly fascinated by their genitals. In particular, she liked the baby inside the mother doll, which she pulled out and put back numerous times within a session. Alicia asked if she could make her own anatomical doll out of cloth. This was a long-term

Figure 6–4. Ten-year-old girl's family portrait

project that took many weeks to complete. Alicia wanted to replicate the mother doll exactly, including a vaginal opening, uterus, and unborn baby, which could be "birthed" repeatedly (see Figure 6–5). She also made clothes for the doll. Once completed, this doll took on an important role in Alicia's therapy. She brought it to therapy sessions, and for a month it became like a transitional object that she carried with her everywhere. Her play with the doll became very specific and frequent. She began birthing the baby doll repeatedly. The motions actually took the form of masturbation, as the doll was pulled out and pushed back into the vaginal opening up to a hundred times within the course of an evening at home, much to the consternation of her houseparents. The houseparents were urged to let the play

Figure 6–5. Ten-year-old girl's self-made anatomical doll

continue as long as it was within the house. This play ulti-mately led to a decrease in her masturbatory behavior, as she was able to gain mastery over these sexual impulses through the substitution of the doll. As with a true transi-tional object, over time the doll lost meaning for her. She left it with the therapist one day and never retrieved it. Shortly thereafter, she left the treatment center to live in a pre-adoptive home. Reportedly, the masturbation behavior did not occur in her new school. Alicia's substitution of the doll for her own sexual acting out was an age-appropriate response dependent upon her achievement of ego activities that were sublimatory, adaptive, and defensive.

Avoidance of sexuality at latency may be seen in the company the child prefers to keep. Generally, girls are more comfortable in the company of girls and boys are more comfortable in the company of boys. Same-sex group therapy, then, becomes an effective therapeutic modality; however, the therapist will need to be attuned to individual children's coping styles and adjust therapeutic goals to fit the needs of each.

Socially, the child no longer operates only in dyadic relationships but proceeds to more complex systems of relationship (Greenspan 1979). At this time, group therapy becomes a key treatment component, for now children can operate within a group system. Initially, the purpose of group therapy is simply to help the child feel less alone with abuse issues. He will not necessarily be ready to empathize with other victims, but will benefit from knowing that others have experienced what he has experienced. Later in latency, however, children become more peer-oriented (at the gang age, from about 9 to 12). Once this happens, the therapist can work with the child on identification with the group. Children can begin to talk to one another within the group, rather than approaching the group as if it were simultaneous individual therapies. At around latency age, children will also be able to employ the development of new affects, such as empathy, in their repertoire of feelings. They will be more able to identify and empathize with one another, and to note similarities and differences between each other's experiences. Altruistic feelings, greater social awareness, intellectual gains that allow for an integration of primary and secondary process thinking, and the employment of judgment and logic to situations, help children gain in stability and mastery of the environment. Thus they can use each other's as well as their own experiences to process feelings and learn appropriate coping responses in potential sexually abusive situations. Drama therapy is a wonderful addition to group sessions at this stage, as it allows children to "try on" different roles and feelings.

At the stage of concrete operations, the child develops the ability to classify. This helps the child to master concepts in mathematics (Piaget and Inhelder 1969, Silver 1990); it also helps him to classify feelings, by both generalizing and discriminating between feelings (Greenspan 1979). Figure 6–6 is an example of some of the complexities of feelings the concrete operational child is capable of articulating.

> The artist, Janice, is the younger of two siblings who were referred for therapy because of their repeated sexual acting-out behavior in the home. Although the 12-year-old was seen as the initiator, Janice, a 7-year-old, was eagerly participating, and was taking the new behavior to school. Janice asked if she could draw what her 12-year-old sister does to her at night. She drew herself in her bed crying. When asked how she feels, she said she feels mad, but then it feels good and sometimes she likes it. I asked her to name all the feelings, and wrote them on the picture for her. She said, "Horrible, stupid, worried, abused, scared, ugly." This session repre-

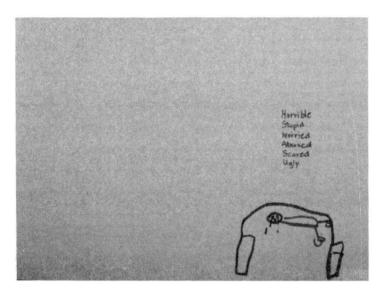

Figure 6–6. Seven-year-old's depiction of how she feels when being sexually abused

sented considerable insight, and the fact that she could identify both liking the abuse and hating it suggested that she was ready to look at her own role in the sexual activity that was occurring.

The child is capable of more advanced understanding of feelings and gradations of feelings, and can understand the concept of feeling several different things at the same time. However, denial is a key defense, so the therapist may need to recognize that talking with the child specifically about what happened to him will not be easy for him at this stage. Janice clearly was ready to talk about her abuse, and used art to help herself process her feelings. Had she not been able to talk so directly, consequences for the sexual acting-out behavior would have been initiated, and psychological education aimed at abuse prevention would have been the focus of therapy. Thus, unless it is particularly relevant for a certain child, the therapist should not be too concerned about pressing for disclosure of details about the abuse as long as the psychological education aimed at preventive skills is completed and consequences are being administered consistently. The child will talk when it is safe for him to talk.

The child takes the first steps toward moral development at this stage, so the concept of right versus wrong can be introduced. The child can see how the behavior can be wrong, and that it does not mean that the child is wrong or bad.

Several weeks later, Janice and I discussed how she has control and can make a decision about sexually acting out with her sister. Janice drew two pictures, one expressing "wrong" thinking and one expressing "right" thinking in regard to making a decision about whether or not to sexually act out (see Figures 6–7 and 6–8). Her "wrong" picture shows her thinking, "I want to. I don't want to. She wants to—I can feel it. Gussie will get mad. I don't want her to get depressed at me. Nah, go ahead and do it." Her "right" picture shows her thinking, "I don't want to. I'll get angry with myself and have to suffer the consequences if I do it. *No!* Leave me alone. I'm going to tell a grown-up." The beginnings of moral development for this child were tenuous, and notice that one of her reasons for not acting out is because "Gussie will get mad. I don't want her to get depressed at me." She has not yet internalized this value, but her picture shows a good beginning with this struggle.

Figure 6–7. Seven-year-old girl's concept of "right" thinking

In terms of psychological education for sexual abuse prevention, at this stage the child can logically understand the meaning behind safety precautions that previously were simply repeated. He can help formulate safety precautions related

Figure 6–8. Seven-year-old girl's concept of "wrong" thinking

specifically to his situation. In this context, children should be able to identify specific persons to whom they could go if in trouble, identify situations in their own lives that are not safe, identify kinds of touch (good, bad, confusing), and identify and take ownership of feelings.

During the previous stage, children were able to repeat stories presented and act them out. Now, the child's ability to move between past and present and make anticipatory images allows him to create his own solutions to a hypothetical situation presented by the therapist. Additionally, he is capable of creating his own scenarios. Therefore, in psychological education groups, children can play act stories of abuse and find their own solutions. For example, anatomical dolls can be used to set up scenarios of potentially abusive situations. The child can then act out different possibilities of coping. The child's ability to make anticipatory images or suggest movements, despite the fact that he has not observed them yet, can be seen in the following case vignette (Klorer 1995).

> Three girls between the ages of 7 and 9 were seen in weekly group therapy. Some psychological education aimed at sexual abuse prevention had been introduced. The sessions were both directive and nondirective, depending upon the goals for a particular week. During nondirective sessions, the girls frequently chose to play with the anatomical dolls because the dolls stimulated their issues of sexuality. The girls began incorporating the dolls into stories. Invariably, the stories revolved around a mean perpetrator sexually abusing a young girl. A policeman would then rescue her. This was a new story, not one that had previously been read to them. The girls would then act out the child's role in prosecution and punishment of the perpetrator, empowering themselves in the process. The children demonstrated their abilities to create a solution to a set problem based upon their own experiences, but one also involving their wish for more power in the resolution.

Therapy at this stage of development will focus on the child's feelings of powerlessness, sexualization, and denial. Expressive therapies are used as a means of helping children express those feelings and issues that are avoided and denied verbally. Expressive work gives them a safe avenue by which to approach the issues, and often precedes verbal disclosure and processing. It is important that the therapist stay with the child's level of denial and support the process of allowing the issues to unfold as he becomes ready to experience them.

ᴅᴄ 7 ᴄᴅ

Too Close for Comfort":
Ages 12 through Adolescence

Alicia, the girl in the previous chapter who made the anatomical doll during her latency period when she was in residential treatment, contacted me at age 17, wanting to re-enter
therapy with me in my private practice. Seven years had
passed since I had seen her. Immediately upon entering the
office, Alicia said it brought back memories of our previous
work. She noticed my anatomical dolls, and talked about the
one she made. I still had her doll and retrieved it from a back
room. She seemed surprised that I had kept it, and said that
I should still keep it. She appeared somewhat regressed, talking haltingly, almost in baby-talk. She looked around my office, comparing things I now had to things I had previously.

At adolescence, Alicia was ready to approach her issues
more directly than she could at latency. When asked what
she wanted to work on in therapy, Alicia said, "I want to work
on my feelings about whether or not I should go live with my

mom. Because I want to, but I think maybe it's not such a good idea." I knew from our previous work that Alicia's mother physically abused Alicia and participated in sexual abuse between Alicia and her stepfather. The next few months of therapy were focused on Alicia's continued expectations that her mother would return her phone calls, and continued sadness and disappointment when her mother did not.

The other issue that emerged for Alicia at adolescence was her promiscuity. At the time I began seeing her at 17, Alicia was having indiscriminate sex with older men, had engaged in a sexual threesome, and was having an affair with a married man.

The adolescent does not repress things as fully as he or she could in latency. At adolescence, the child is typically bombarded with issues of sexuality, identity formation, and relationship finding. Or, to use a more current expression typical of this age, at adolescence "the shit hits the fan."

The normal sexual urges that appear at adolescence are exacerbated by the sexually abused child's previous experience. The abused child may already have been engaging in sexual behavior throughout development. Consequently, she may have a skewed viewpoint on appropriate sexual encounters. Adolescents who equate sex with love will describe promiscuous behavior as if the attention bestowed meant they were loved, and will not think in terms of how the promiscuity may not in fact be meeting any of their emotional needs.

DEVELOPMENTAL ISSUES

At this time, the child gradually moves into the stage of formal operations, which is characterized by the adolescent's ability to deal with hypothetical and more abstract situations. This developmental milestone opens up numerous possibilities for therapeutic processing.

In terms of art development, the child at this age moves into the Age of Reasoning, or the Pseudo-Naturalistic Stage. Most people stop growing in their art development at this age unless they seek out more professional coursework, so adolescent art is similar to adult art in style. However the content and emotion in the art often betrays the adolescent's developmental struggles and issues. Typically at this stage there is a decrease in spontaneous art activity and the beginning of more critical thinking in terms of art products. The adolescent attempts to draw naturalistically and to depict what can be seen. The adolescent also becomes aware of perspective and the horizon line when drawing landscapes (Lowenfeld and Brittain 1987).

Just as girls develop earlier physically, so do they show greater interest in drawing the human figure than boys do. Sexual characteristics of drawings at this stage can be greatly overexaggerated and still be within the normal range, reflective of the adolescent's concern over her own physical changes. Adolescents strive for greater naturalism in their figure drawings, including joints, folds in clothing, and attention to details such as hairstyle and makeup on figures (Lowenfeld and Brittain 1987). At the same time, adolescents develop an increased ability to draw abstractly, and are able to represent some of the intangible feelings that often bubble to the surface unsolicited.

According to Greenspan (1979), this stage of development includes the capacity for understanding inverse and reciprocal relationships, and the ability to relate groups of variables to one another. Adolescents can solve more complex problems with many sets of variables. The adolescent's ability to think hypothetically in terms of what is probable frees her from the frightening nature of feelings. The adolescent is aware of many available options. The adolescent can weigh the consequences of aggression, sexuality, and other such matters and make conscious decisions accordingly (Greenspan 1979).

THE CHILD'S UNDERSTANDING OF TRAUMA

Preadolescent and adolescent children now confront sexual issues as a natural course of development. Children who had previously terminated therapy often come back at this time because suddenly they find themselves needing to approach issues that can no longer be avoided. The adolescent may be more ready now to talk about sex. In fact, budding sexuality and hormones may make sex a preoccupation.

Memories that may have been successfully repressed emerge at adolescence, stimulated by the developmental tasks that come with the age.

> Despite her wish to go home, Alicia was able to reconnect with feelings about what it was like when she lived with her mother. "She's an alcoholic who married an abusive man, my stepdad. He beat her all the time. He sexually abused me. He still hasn't admitted that he did it." No longer did Alicia repress memories of the abuse. She weighed this information against her attachment feelings toward her mother, and the desire to go home appeared to be winning out over her memories of abuse.

It is impossible to talk about adolescent development without mentioning the psychological ramifications of rapprochement involved in this period. At adolescence, the child goes through a second individuation and rapprochement period that in many ways is worse than the first, the "terrible two's." The adolescent is still emotionally tied to the parent and may be dependent upon the parent for satisfaction of physical needs, such as food and shelter, yet is compelled to make the transition into adult independence and individuation. Separation from parental figures, which is the business of adolescence, can have extreme ramifications for the abused child, whose separation issues have perhaps already been complicated by confused relational boundaries. The betrayal of relationship boundaries remains one of the most traumatic and difficult issues to address therapeutically. However, at adolescence the child acquires the ability to process hypothetical relational issues more directly.

Blos (1962) sees development of object relations as the pivotal problem of a "normal" adolescence, with the solution depending upon the many variations this theme undergoes over the years. During adolescence, the child must detach from the parents (along with siblings and parent substitutes). The adolescent becomes concerned with object relinquishment and object finding. A complication in the area of attachment issues occurs when the parent or parent substitute actually was a sexual object. When Blos speaks of renunciation of the primary love objects as sexual objects, he is speaking hypothetically. When there is a confused relational boundary because of sexual abuse, this detachment, which is so necessary before a nonincestuous object choice can be made, is a tremendous leap for the adolescent to make. From a therapeutic standpoint, it can remain a prominent issue throughout life.

Think now about Alicia, who wants to go back to mother, not separate from her. For such a child, who is still trying to please and win the affection of the parent, detachment cannot happen. Therefore, attachment to another also cannot happen. That becomes a primary issue, as Alicia's desire to re-enter therapy suggests, at precisely the time when developmental tasks appropriate to a given stage are challenged.

TREATMENT ISSUES

Some therapy goals for the adolescent at this stage are to (1) form a therapeutic, trusting relationship with the therapist; (2) use therapy to talk about sexual urges and learn appropriate strategies for dealing with these urges; (3) explore feelings surrounding past rejections and abuse and make connections between past and current relationships; and (4) help the child to define future goals and set attainable short-term goals for herself in order to recognize successes. Other treatment goals will need to be individualized for particular clients.

The adolescent consolidates an integrated and organized representation of herself in relation to past, present, and future. Understanding and integrating a variety of variables, including discordant ones, helps the adolescent rectify identity issues (Greenspan 1979).

A collage entitled *How I See Myself* brought forth a number of insights related to her past for 15-year-old Shelly (see Figure 7–1). She found the words "Underneath it all, she's a skilled actress," which she said related to herself becoming an actress when she got sexually abused, and her feeling now that she is very good at it. The phrase "Too close for comfort" related to her not liking to get close to people,

Figure 7–1. Collage self-portrait by 15-year-old Shelly

which she connected to past hurts. The words "Running away" led to an insight that she does not run to anything or away from anything, but just runs. These insights, which pulled together past with present, helped this adolescent continue her quest through identity issues.

Trust becomes a major therapeutic issue that is dealt with in the transference and in the sessions directly. The adolescent may attempt to set up power struggles, which should be avoided at all costs. A good rule when working therapeutically with an adolescent is never to ask a question to which the child may lie in response. In other words, never ask things like, "Are you sexually active?" or "Do you do drugs?" If the child answers in a lie, it sets up a precedent that therapy is not truthful. A therapist can talk about any issue without ever asking the question. More often than not, when approached without being asked the question, the adolescent volunteers the information. The trust that is established in the course of therapy will be one of the curative factors. For children who have been lied to and betrayed in other ways, this trust and honesty is one of the most difficult things to establish.

This leads back to the idea that in abuse cases it is the betrayal of the relationship that is the deepest part of the wound. The child has long since gotten over the physical scars and trauma, but the betrayals, lies, and mixed messages cannot be easily overcome. The betrayal has taught the child not to dare to trust, for fear of being hurt. It also teaches her to actively avoid intense emotional relationships for fear of the pain evoked by them.

Shelly phoned her mother from the group home where she has lived for the past four years, hoping that perhaps her mother would want her now. During the course of the conversation, her mother told her she wished Shelly had never been born. Shelly took a knife and slashed at her forearms that weekend, causing multiple superficial wounds. Several weeks later, in group art therapy, the directive was for each of the four girls to create a "self symbol." Shelly drew a heart with a knife in it (see Figure 7–2) and disclosed that she was sexually abused throughout her early years, and was gang-raped at knifepoint at age 12. "I tried to forget it for a long time. I won't ever trust because I trusted once before and got burned." Shelly protects herself from ever feeling the pain by

Figure 7–2. Fifteen-year-old Shelly's self symbol

not getting attached. She numbs herself from feelings, but then she creates physical pain by cutting.

When a child is engaging in self-mutilation while numbed from emotional pain, the first thing the therapist needs to do is find a place where the feelings inside *can* be expressed. Adolescents often write poetry because it offers some distance to their emotions. For adolescents who have difficulty verbalizing, this kind of an outlet can be safer.

The place where Shelly appears to be able to get in touch with her feelings in an appropriate way is through poetry and art. She writes painful poems of her deep feelings and fears. About once a month she delivers a stack of poetry to her group therapy members, which is her way of connecting with them. She is unable to talk about these poems.

Can you keep a secret, if I tell you what I feel?
Can you keep a secret, if I tell you this is real?
Can you keep a secret and promise not to laugh?
Will you understand if I tell you that it hurts?
Will you hold my hand if I tell you what is wrong?
Will you say I lie, even as I cry?
Will you be angry if I make a mistake?
Will you understand if I tell you there's not much more I
   can take? . . .
Are you strong enough to understand and still believe in me?
Will you laugh, tease, and run if I tell you that I bleed?
Can you keep a secret, if I tell you of the past?
Will you still be around, will the friendship last? . . .
Can you keep a secret if I tell you why I cry?
Will you understand that I need you by my side? . . .
Can you keep a secret, if I tell you how I see?
Will you try to understand, and still believe in me?

The fact that Shelly has this outlet for her inner feelings
makes the prognosis better than if she were totally numbing
herself from all feelings and only using self-mutilation to feel.
That she can touch and put words on her feelings through
poetry gives the therapist a place from which to begin working with her. Through her poetry, she experiments with sharing what is inside. When it is accepted, not only by the therapist but by her other group members, she is encouraged to
continue this self exploration. Her primary art modality is
collage, and she makes collages both in art therapy and at
home. This process allows her to cut. She finds images and
words in magazines that relate to her own issues, and she
communicates them safely through this method.

Group therapy is a key strategy in working with adolescents. Often, they can help each other more than the therapist can help them. Sharing feelings, processing relationships and sexual issues, making connections between past and present behavior, and identifying with the group helps adolescents sort through their conflicting feelings.

The need to form a gender identity challenges the adolescent to face sexuality issues. At this stage, she is capable of making connections between an abusive past and her present sexuality, as exemplified by 14-year-old Ginny.

Ginny came into therapy one week complaining of menstrual cramps, which led to her drawing an abstract picture about being female and having periods. She drew pain, and drew what she termed the cycles of the day. "It begins okay, then there is pain, there is embarrassment, and then it's okay again at night." This led into a second abstract picture about female sexuality and disclosure of past abuse. The pastel drawing, which symbolized her life as being colorful and happy up until age 9, shows a diagonal slash over a rainbow, which she said was indicative of her trauma. As she drew, Ginny disclosed that when she was 9 her mother owed someone money for drugs and sold her daughter for sex to pay the debt. A large brown penis and hand extend into the right of the picture frame. She was able to talk about her current feelings about sexuality and the effect that the abuse has on her now. She said she was confused, embarrassed, angry, and had difficulty with trust and hate. She titled the picture, *Trust at Eight, Hatred at Nine* (Figure 7–3). Ginny also talked about her recent pelvic exam, and said that she "leaves her body" to get through it. This awareness of her

Figure 7–3. Fourteen-year-old's depiction of the effects of sexual abuse, titled *Trust at Eight, Hatred at Nine*

ability to dissociate suggests that she has defense mechanisms that worked well for her and that continue to be called upon when necessary. Her advanced understanding of her own sexuality comes with the maturity of adolescence.

Dissociation, which in the past may have been symptomatic, is used as a barometer of a good defense structure when it can be called upon to assist the client in dealing with stress. The fact that this adolescent is aware of its use, but is not a slave to it, suggests her maturity and health. She can now talk about the trauma and use art to abstractly represent feelings evoked by it.

At this stage of development, the adolescent can integrate many concepts that formerly eluded her. For example, feelings about a perpetrator can be processed in a more sophisticated way. The adolescent can assign multiple feelings to the same person, can hypothesize why the perpetrator acted as such, and can assimilate past, present and future; thus she is not held to the fear and helplessness felt previously but is more able to fantasize how she would handle a future encounter. With this ability, she can integrate what happened in the past with present reality and can use this information to formulate future ideals.

The adolescent can also process her own behavior in a more sophisticated way. For a child who is acting out inappropriately, the issues can be dealt with directly, once a relationship based upon honesty has been established. Issues do not need to be couched in metaphor or expressed symbolically.

> Twelve-year-old Johanna was asked to draw how she felt while sexually acting out, and how she felt now. Her picture, Figure 7–4, suggests a multitude of feelings occurring at the same time, and an ability to see how feelings change, hypothetically discriminating between feelings then and feelings now. "How I felt then" includes "wanting, good, yearning, needing, hoping, having fun, willing, trusting, and praying." "How I feel now" includes "guilty, silly, dumb, stupid, letting down, mad, sad, uneasy, and scared."

This same ability to integrate feelings and actions can help the sexually acting-out adolescent to assimilate new coping skills by identifying past situations that caused her to act out, and to formulate new solutions to those situations.

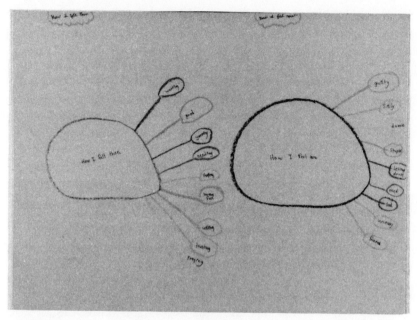

Figure 7–4. Twelve-year-old female's picture of how she felt before and after engaging in sexual perpetrating behavior

I asked Johanna to think about what kinds of situations stimulated her to act out sexually with her younger sister, and to draw a picture of hypothetical solutions (see Figure 7–5). The situation she drew involved herself hearing her mother and mother's boyfriend having sex during the night. This would stimulate Johanna's sexual urges and would cause her to go to her sister's bed and initiate sexual activity. The picture shows her standing outside the door and thinking, "Why do they do it so long? Don't they know how to sleep? Why do they make those noises? I wish they would stop! They are going to break the bed down! They always do that! He is hitting mommy! I'm knocking on the door."

Figure 7–5. Twelve-year-old's picture of what stimulates her sexual behavior

Her solutions, derived with my help, were to close the door and turn on the radio, read a book, or masturbate instead of acting out with her sister. This picture also made me aware of the need to work with the mother on more discretion in her sexual activity. The child's ability to fantasize how she would handle a future encounter helped her to strategize and take responsibility for her own treatment. The child and I became team members.

Sexual acting out is a normal developmental progression that occurs during adolescence, and the child who wishes to act out sexually can usually find willing partners. However, a distinction needs to be made between sexual behavior that is consensual and that which is coerced. Consequences for perpetrating or coercion become even more severe. The parental figure or person who discovers the perpetrating behavior needs to up the ante of the consequence and give a clear message that any perpetrating behavior will not be tolerated. It is no longer enough to use time-outs and withdrawal of privileges. The police and/or child-abuse hotline should be called for any perpetrating behavior, particularly if it occurs with a younger child.

In the case of consensual sexual behavior, the rules become unclear for the adolescent. It is a time to begin talking about sex, choices, relationships, and promiscuity, and the consequences of disease and pregnancy. For the first time, the adolescent begins making choices about sexual relationships.

During preadolescence and early adolescence, relationships with the opposite sex become a key issue. In the normal course of development, these relationships are often fleeting, as the child is experimenting with codes of behavior, trust, sexuality, and dependency versus autonomy. During later adolescence, intimacy and object choice become more important. The child may be ready to explore why he or she chooses partners who are abusive, indifferent, or losers. The child may form indiscriminate attachments, moving from abusive relationship to abusive relationship. This was true in the case of Edna.

Edna was sexually abused by her father beginning at age 3. Now, at age 14, she asks why every boy she gets involved with is "such a jerk," yet she continues to choose boyfriends who lie to her, cheat, and disrespect her, and the focus of her relationships is primarily sexual. Edna and Shelly are in group therapy, and both ask the same question: "Why are guys such assholes?" Another group member, further along in her treatment, asks, "No, why are we attracted to such assholes?"

Sexually abused girls will fantasize about getting pregnant, which ties in with intimacy issues. The search for love often compels the adolescent female to create someone who will love her. This dilemma is poignantly illustrated in the poems and pictures created by Jessica.

Jessica, age 20, was referred for therapy because of her inability to take on some of the adult roles that her placement in a semi-independent living program required. She was doing poorly in school, was having problems with relationships with men, and had periodic depressive episodes. As a child, Jessica was sexually abused by her mother's boyfriend, which her mother denied. She was physically and emotionally abused by her mother, and at age 12 her mother cruelly abandoned her, telling her that no one would ever love her. Jessica had been in foster care since age 12. Throughout her years of foster homes and residential treatment, she had intermittent contact with her mother. No matter how unavailable her mother continued to be and despite a separation of three hundred miles, Jessica continually attempted to please her mother and was continually hurt. Although she could intellectually assess her mother accurately, she was emotionally tied to her and could not separate. Her fear of rejection permeated all of her relationships. She pushed people who might care for her away, and consequently was involved in relationships with men that were unsatisfying, of short duration, and led to depressive episodes.

She also yearned for a commitment with a boyfriend, and she talked about this frequently in therapy. Jessica's illustration of this need (see Figure 7–6) betrayed her actual fear of commitment. "Commitment" is represented by a large black obstacle, and during this session she acknowledged her fear of committing to a boyfriend, to school, and to other friends.

Jessica's solution was to have a baby. Her picture of this wish (see Figure 7–7) and an accompanying poem, attested to her longing for the love she never felt. Ironically, she titled this series *The Child in All of Us,* suggesting that on some level she knew that the desire to have a child stemmed from the desire to be nurtured herself.

Figure 7–6. Twenty-year-old's abstraction, titled
Commitment

Figure 7–7. Twenty-year-old's picture of a wish for a baby, titled, *The Child In All of Us*

Thus, the cycle continues. Now she is a single young woman with a child and is having difficulty bonding with her baby. The key issue, attachment and rejection, having never been resolved, haunts her still. She questions why she cannot love. She realizes, too late, that the baby cannot meet her many needs. Jessica will not be able to completely resolve her issues with attachment until she can resolve her primary attachment with her mother and the rejection that is intertwined with her inner self. When her mother calls to tell her she is sick, Jessica rushes to her side. Perhaps now she will love me, Jessica hopes.

«© 8 ©»

"My Heart Bleeds for Harmony": Involving the Family in Therapy¹

Bridget, age 10, was brought to therapy by her mother, who defined "the problem" with Bridget as being her temper tantrums. Her mother wanted me to do an attitude and behavior change. During our second evaluative session, I asked Bridget to draw her version of "the problem" (see Figure 8–1). Bridget divided the page into four sections and drew her problem with each family member. She felt that her "problem" with mother's boyfriend was her fear of him, now that the family had moved into his home, based upon mother's previous choices in men. Her problem with her brother was that they fight too much. The problem with herself was that

---

1. I am indebted to James Consoli (1956–1997), M. A., A.T.R., for many of the ideas presented in this chapter. Although we never published our research, we co-presented our six years of collaborative work at conferences of the American Art Therapy Association.

she shows her anger "and half the time I don't know what I'm angry about." Her problem with her mother was "mom doing drugs at crack houses." She described her mother as being gone for days at a time and the two children fending for themselves, "worrying about whether she is dead or alive."

Typically, I ask children after each individual session if there is anything they would like to share with the parent or guardian. Then, when we bring the parent in at the end of the session, the child has already decided whether to have the artwork displayed or put away. In this way, I am allowing the child to control what is talked about with the parent. Bridget wanted to share the picture, but wanted to cover up the section about mother's boyfriend because she did not want to hurt his feelings. However, when mother and her boyfriend came in, Bridget talked about his section as well as the others and cried when she explained the part about her mother.

In this session it was clearly communicated that I needed to do family therapy, rather than colluding with the mother and keeping Bridget the assigned "problem."

Sometimes a child is referred for therapy because of his inappropriate behavior at home or school. The identified client may have been the one brought to therapy, but one cannot ignore the family system from which he emerged. In many situations, if the issues are not addressed within the family context, the prognosis is guarded to poor. The therapist must understand how the family system may contribute to or even require the acting-out behavior from a child who has been identified as the "problem."

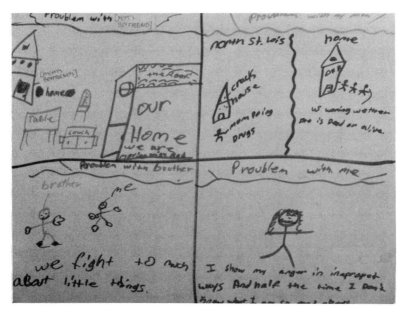

Figure 8–1. Ten-year-old Bridget's picture of "the problem" in her family

Work with children is more complex than simply following a family systems approach, however. As much as the therapist may see the problem as being family-based, there may not be a consistent family with whom to work. Often in work with children, the child's living situation is not predictable and will change over the course of treatment. A foster home placement may be disrupted because of the child's behavior, and this may result in a series of unsuccessful placements for the child until the behavior is controlled. In divorce cases, custody arrangements may change. A pre-adoptive home may fail. A therapist may be working with a child in foster care, and then suddenly parental rights have been terminated, and the child is available for adoption. All of these changes will affect the direction of therapy.

The therapist may have to straddle the different paradigms of perceiving the problem from the intrapsychic and family systems perspectives. When family therapy is deemed appropriate, the therapist must formulate an understanding of the family group as a whole as it struggles with individual needs and relationships and with the difficulty of balancing one person's expression of internal object relations with those of others (Scharff 1989, Scharff and Scharff, 1991, Sussal 1992). Issues of attachment and separation continue in both paradigms.

INVOLVING THE PARENT OR GUARDIAN IN THE CHILD'S INDIVIDUAL THERAPY

It is almost impossible to work with children without involving the parent or guardian in the therapy in some way. The level of involvement will vary, but some cooperation is necessary even to begin therapy, as a parent or other significant adult is required at least for transportation, unless it is provided by a protective services agency.

The minimal level of involvement, then, is relying on the parent or guardian not to sabotage the child's individual therapy. Some communication with the guardian is necessary to understand any destructive acts that might impede the progress of therapy. Jealousy of the therapist's relationship with the child is one possible impediment, and this possibility should be addressed at the beginning of the process. The parents might be reminded that, unlike them, the therapist never has to ask the child to do dishes or math homework. Children often show great pleasure in coming to an expressive therapist's office because, being stocked with art materials and toys and bright colors, it looks and feels like fun. Parents who feel that the purpose of therapy is not to be fun, but to confront the child about behaviors, may not understand the office or the relationship. Helping them to realize that the relationship the therapist builds with the child will be very different from the one the parent has with the child will reassure the parents and enlist their cooperation and support.

Suspiciousness about the therapeutic process can also be a factor. The therapist must be sensitive to the differing values that clients may have, and that the idea of "therapy" is not accepted in all families or all cultures.

There is no universal, cross-cultural definition as to what constitutes "child abuse." Sometimes a family is brought to the attention of the authorities when, in their own culture, the behavior would be considered normal parental discipline. Forming a therapeutic alliance in such cases is possible but is often very difficult. Because of cultural differences, it may take much longer to build the kind of trust that is necessary. Helping the parent understand the processes of the child protection agency and the legal system is a good place to begin.

Attempting to include the parent in formulating treatment goals can be helpful in allying with the parent. Most important, the parent cannot feel blamed because of the child's problems. Empathic statements suggesting how difficult things must be for the parent can help the parent feel supported.

If the therapist is working individually with a child, the more the therapist can tell the parent about the process of therapy, the better. Demystifying therapy requires as much open communication as possible without compromising the child's confidentiality. The parents need to know that, although the therapist cannot tell them exactly what a child says, the therapist will attempt to tell them how he feels and help them to understand why he is acting the way he is. Ideally, the parent and therapist become team members in support of the child's mental health and growth.

ASSESSMENT OF FAMILIES THROUGH ART

An assessment of the child referred to therapy may reveal that he is acting out the family's dysfunction and if this is so, therapy will have little impact unless the entire family is involved. Assessing an entire family through art is one way to establish a sense of each person's role in the family and how these roles are intertwined. Of course, family art evaluations require that the entire family participate, and families are not always willing to do so, just as they do not always support a child's individual therapy. However, the addition of art to the assessment process can make it seem less threatening and take the parents off their guard.

The traditional family art evaluation was designed by Kwiatkowska (1978), and consists of a series of six drawings done by the entire family. The drawings are designed to assess both intrapsychic and interpersonal issues that can be helpful in looking at intergenerational patterns. The drawings, in order, consist of: (1) free choice, (2) family portrait, (3) abstract family portrait, (4) scribble, which is then made into a picture, (5) joint family scribble, and (6) free choice. The joint family scribble is created by everyone together on one eighteen by twenty-four inch piece of paper so that the therapist can observe family interactions, boundaries, and roles.

Landgarten (1987) also recognized the power of the non-verbal art task in her drawing assessment series. Landgarten asks the family to participate in three drawing tasks: (1) non-verbal team art task, (2) nonverbal family art task, and (3) verbal family art task. These tasks are designed to assess the family system, including ego strengths and weaknesses, roles and behavioral patterns, modes of communication, power and control, and the family's overall style of interaction.

Other art therapists (Linesch 1993, Riley 1985, 1987, 1988, 1993, Sobol 1982) have expanded upon the work of Kwiatkowska and use slightly different or ongoing family art assessments. The interactions that occur within the family art evaluation are a repetition of what happens at home. The same dyads, triads, power struggles and conflicts will emerge through the process. The family art evaluation helps the therapist identify a family's strengths, and thus allows the therapist to design a treatment plan relating to the issues presented and capitalizing on the available strengths.

The P. family brought their two young children into therapy because a baby-sitter had fondled the children. Another therapist had told them their children would never get over the trauma, and the parents were seeking a second opinion because they felt that this gloom-and-doom approach was too strong in light of what had happened; yet they were conscientious enough to want to be sure. The abuse involved a baby-sitter that the children loved, and although the children were confused, they were not exhibiting signs of trauma in their behavior. An art therapy assessment with the entire family revealed a delightful, playful family with many strengths. The 7-year-old's family portrait drawing (see Figure 8–2) suggested an

Figure 8–2. Seven-year-old's family portrait

imaginative, intelligent child with good ego strength and high self-esteem. She drew a silly picture that both children found hilarious. She said she drew her mom standing on her head, her brother was drawn with "boogers" coming out of his nose, her dad was flying through the air on a zip wire, and she depicted herself jumping out of a tree. The broad use of color and spontaneity in the picture were suggestive of her cheerful disposition and sense of humor, which was shared by other family members. There were no signs of extreme anxiety, excessive sexuality, or stress in any of the other family members' pictures, and there were no behavioral manifestations of anxiety in the session or reported at home. However, it was apparent in the pictures and in the family's interactions that home life could be chaotic and that the children sometimes ran the household with their shenanigans. The parents did not seem to know when to provide structure. Further discussion with the parents revealed that things like bedtime became long ordeals of children testing limits, with parents ending up feeling frustrated and angry at their lack of control. I recommended that the parents attend just a few sessions to work on establishing clearer boundaries with their children. Like many parents today, they were operating under the misguided notion that disciplining children will harm their self-esteem. As I pointed out through the pictures, however, I was not at all worried about these children's self-esteem. They drew themselves as large or larger than their parents and in positions of power. I was concerned about structure and safety. These issues were easily addressed in a few sessions with the parents, who were highly motivated to live in less chaos. To address the sexual abuse, I lent the parents several books on sexual abuse prevention skills and asked them to read the books to the children at home. In this way, the parents would be helping the children see that what happened was wrong, but would not be catastrophizing it. The assumption that the children had been traumatized could easily have been played out through years of therapy, yet the strengths evident through the family art evaluation suggested it was unnecessary. My recommendation to the parents was to watch the children's behavior. They would know, through behavioral manifestations, when to bring the children into therapy.

Therapists should receive training in art therapy before attempting a family art evaluation, as the dynamics of the family can be swiftly brought to the surface through this nonverbal process and the clinician should be armed with appropriate interventions to defuse the situation. Art can be a very power-ful tool, eliciting a multitude of repressed or unconscious feel-ings, and families can be quite fragile. Often, it is the joint fam-ily scribble that becomes the most revealing of the family's precariousness.

> Figure 8–3, titled *My Heart Bleeds for Harmony*, reflects a family's plea for help. The identified client, an 11-year-old incest victim, titled it and made most of the decisions in the drawing, while her mother criticized and obliterated much of her work and her stepfather (not the perpetrator) sat dispassionately and stared out the window. The family art evaluation revealed communication patterns, issues surrounding boundaries and roles, and decision-making processes. Through this picture, the focus shifted from the identified client to the family as a system, and treatment goals that involved the entire family were formulated. The theme in this picture was repeated numerous times in art therapy with this family.

FAMILY THERAPY IN DIVORCING FAMILIES

Divorcing parents seek out therapy for their children for a num-ber of reasons. A child may develop behavior problems in reac-tion to the stress between the parents. Sometimes children do this to divert the parents' attention away from their own fights. It is the child's way of controlling the stress in the household. Sudden changes in a child's behavior alert the parents that he too is experiencing the effects of the divorce. The child may be mourning the loss of family as he has always known it, and he may not know what to do with these feelings. The parents may

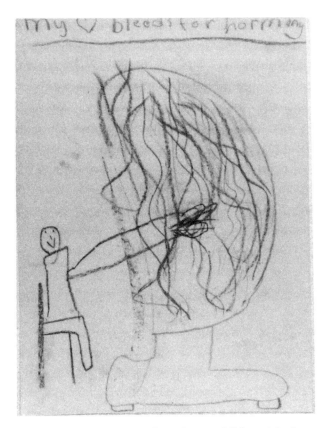

Figure 8–3. Joint family scribble, titled
My Heart Bleeds for Harmony

decide to take a proactive stance and use therapy to help the children process their feelings about the divorce. Therapy can also be used to help parents set up realistic expectations for the children and themselves in regard to sharing custodial chores, discipline, and traditional family events.

An expressive therapist's approach to a family going through divorce will likely include an evaluative period that includes a family art evaluation of some kind, if both parents are cooperative. In particular, obtaining each person's drawing of the family will be helpful in understanding how each family member perceives the family. As in every other situation when a family comes to therapy, there is no prescribed set of rules, and no certain art tasks are required. The therapist will want to individualize the session for the family at hand, choosing drawings that will be most helpful to this particular situation.

> Mrs. T. initially brought in her 5-year-old daughter, Donna, for individual art therapy because of Donna's extremely violent temper tantrums. These tantrums only occurred at home, and mostly with her mother. Donna would hit, scratch, and kick her mother when she did not get her way. She was doing very well in school and had no interactive problems with peers. A brief social history revealed that the parents were in the midst of a divorce. Although the parents felt it was as amicable a divorce as possible, it was clear in the first session that Donna could see nothing good about the upcoming changes in her family. I asked Donna to draw a number of pictures in her first individual session, trying to assess her feelings. When asked directly about her feelings about the changes in her family, Donna said, "We're still going to be a family . . . We're still going to go on family vacations . . . I feel like this—sad and mad . . . I cried when my mom told me about it." Donna's sandtray picture also revealed the turmoil she was feeling inside. Her story was "a wedding. Batman was getting married and some other people were getting married. There was a witch there. Everything—the doghouse, houses, the cemetery—was safe, ex-

cept the wedding. The witch was going to spoil the party." It seemed that Donna was blaming her mother for spoiling her own party, and hence her mother was getting the brunt of Donna's anger. A family art evaluation was the next step in terms of assessment, as clearly this was a family problem that needed to be resolved within the family structure. The pictures requested of the two parents and Donna were (1) a family portrait, (2) feelings about the family changes, and (3) something you would like to tell the others. These were designed to help understand this particular family's means of coping with the stress of the divorce, and assess how they were communicating with each other. For "something you would like to tell the others" Mrs. T. drew an angry picture and said she did not express her own anger. Mr. T. exhibited denial. He drew a picture of the family together, and said, "We'll still be a family." Donna's picture was titled *Sad and Mad*, and revealed that she was expressing anger for the entire family. Interventions and goals were formulated. We agreed that the parents would come to some sessions as a couple so that some issues that they still needed to decide upon as a couple could be negotiated. Donna would be seen individually, so that she could express some of her anger in a safe way. In this case, family therapy was not the modality of choice, as I did not want to collude in the underlying denial that the family would still be a family.

In situations of divorce, there may be a custody battle afoot involving allegations of child abuse, which should be a red flag for the therapist to be extremely careful in making assumptions or "believing" the parent who brings the child in for treatment.

There are sometimes ulterior motives behind bringing children to therapy when there is a custody battle going on; on more than one occasion I have seen a parent appear crestfallen upon being told the good news that I do *not* think the child was abused. It is helpful in such cases to see each parent individually and alone with the child before making any recommendations.

FAMILY THERAPY FOR ISSUES OF GRIEF AND LOSS

When a family has experienced a loss, the children look to the parent to find out how to grieve. Ideally, the grief is handled in a way that allows for individual expression of the multitude of feelings that come with loss, and therapy may not be necessary. In many instances, loss brings a family closer together. In some families, children learn that they must grieve silently. There may be an unstated need to protect a particular family member who is seen as too fragile to handle the grief, so the grief is not expressed. If the loss is through death of a sibling or parent, one child may attempt to take the place of the deceased person, at the expense of his own individuality and autonomy. In cases where the loss has been accompanied by a trauma, such as a murder, there may be a post-traumatic stress component that complicates the child's ability to move through the grieving stages.

Ideally, there is someone attending to the needs of the children when a family experiences loss. Family therapy is one way to address these needs. This may be brief therapy with a definite focus and structured tasks to help the family through the grieving process, or the therapist may take a more open-ended approach to see where the family needs to go with their grief.

Mr. K. brought his three children into therapy because they had witnessed the murder of their mother. The murder had occurred several years prior to his seeking out therapy, yet he felt that the family had not moved beyond what he considered a normal grieving process. He noted that the children were continuing to have anger-management and attention-seeking behavior problems in school and at home, and that these behaviors had not been present before the murder. During the first family session, I asked each family member to draw three pictures: (1) a free choice picture, (2) a picture of your family, and (3) a free choice picture, although "it could be something about your mom." I was interested in knowing how each person would deal with the deceased family member in the family drawing. As I suspected, the children all drew their mother in the family picture. The children asked their father why he did not include the mother, and one child rationalized that "he didn't have room." The father said it was because their mother was dead. At this point, the children immediately engaged in avoidant behavior. One child put his picture on his head, and said "It's raining!" The other two did the same, and soon they were all giggling and singing, "It's raining! It's raining!" In the final drawing, the one that "could be something about your mom," one child drew himself, another child wrote the names of everyone in the family (including the mother's), and one child drew a shape and then said, "I forgot what it's called" (it was a heart). It seemed apparent that these children needed to find a way to talk about and grieve their deceased mother. Family therapy goals were formulated to give the children an opportunity to talk about the murder and help them grieve the loss by making a book about their mother. The book included positive memories of their mother, what happened the day she was murdered, the funeral, and pictures of the family since the murder. Through this process, they also found a way to conceptualize their mother in their pictures. The solution the children came up with was to put their mother inside of a heart, because "she will always be in our hearts."

COURT-ORDERED FAMILY THERAPY

In certain situations the court may order a family into therapy. Although this ensures their physical presence during the hour, it is a less than ideal way to begin the therapeutic relationship. Parents in this situation are often resentful and angry at the invasion into their lives, and then are not willing to invest in the process. Even if the therapist has no formal connection to the child protective services or juvenile court, the suspiciousness with which the clients approach the therapy can be an impediment to any real progress. This can lead to "pretend therapy" (Ackerman et al. 1991).

Ackerman and colleagues (1991) recommend that the therapist's first job be that of differentiating the therapist's self from the protective services agency by not assuming that the family needs treatment, getting to know them as people rather than as an abusive family, and pointing out that the "problem" may be attributable to a lack of understanding with the protective services agency. Such a task needs to be done without splitting and without colluding with the clients in their denial. The therapist must bridge the gap between the protective services worker and the family and help the family to develop a less authoritarian, less adversarial, and more constructive relationship (MacKinnon and James 1992b). The therapist must dance between having an alliance with the family and functioning as part of an overall treatment team on the family's behalf.

Mr. and Mrs. M. were told that if they wanted their children to come back home they had better be involved in therapy. The six children were put into several different foster homes because the house the family was living in had been condemned. The referral came from the child protective agency that removed the children from the home, so immediately there was a suspiciousness about my motives and ability to be objective since I was perceived as part of the system that put their children into foster care. When I went into the waiting room to greet the parents, Mrs. M. sat with her arms folded against her chest, unmoving, and said she came against her will. Her husband was much more willing to play the game of therapy. I spent the first session empathizing with how terrible it must have been for them to have their children pulled away so suddenly, and how traumatic both for the parents and the children. I also emphasized that, although they might feel as if they had no choice about being in therapy, they could choose their own therapist. I encouraged them to interview several therapists so that they could feel more in control. So that they would have a better sense of what art therapy would be like and could then decide whether or not to keep coming, I suggested that the following week they bring their six children and we could do a family art evaluation. This made sense to them. The following week I requested from each family member (1) a free choice drawing, (2) a family drawing, and (3) a picture of "the problem." The last picture revealed that the mother was right. Being put into foster care was much more traumatic for the children than was the condemned house. All of the children seemed to have a good relationship with their parents and looked to them for support and approval. The children missed being a family and did not understand the separation. In the next session, again with just the parents, we talked about the family art evaluation. I pointed out strengths in the family, and then we talked about each child individually. I said that we had to figure out how we might work together to get their children back for good so that the system would leave them alone, as being in foster care was very stressful for the children. Our job was to show the court that they were wrong to take the children. What would it take to get them to see this? The parents had an overwhelming list of physical things that had to be fixed in the house, and we prioritized a few things. Mr. M. was doing the work, but we talked about Mrs. M. taking a more active role in fixing things as well. She did not have her husband's expertise, but she was anxious to learn. He did not think a woman should do this kind of work, however, so getting them to function as a team became our first goal. This goal coincided with parenting skills. I noticed that they did not always function as a team in family decisions. The children split them apart even with simple things that occurred during the evaluation, such as the youngest child asking both parents if it was okay to wash her hands when she did not like the first answer she got. The children were quite rambunctious, and there was little imposition of discipline. Then we talked about each child individually and what we might do in therapy to bring out more self-confidence in one, relieve the oldest child of some of the pressure he apparently carried for the family, and help the youngest child to be expressive, since she kept things buried. We also talked about setting more limits for the children, and the need for the parents to model positive, supportive interactions with each other. Within a month, the children were allowed to go back home. We then worked more specifically on family interactions, boundaries, and setting limits. I designed art directives that would put the parents in a position with more power than the children, trying to strengthen the parental dyad. For example, in one session I asked them to draw their house on large mural paper. The children wanted to rush into this project. I insisted that the parents be the ones to provide the structure for the task and draw the boundaries of the house, and organize the children to fill in the details, setting up the metaphor of what I hoped they would do at home. We also set up a behavior chart to help the parents monitor the children's behavior. By the end of six months of therapy, Mrs. M. did not want to terminate our relationship. She had grown to rely on the therapy for support in dealing with her children's behavior and in being a team player with her husband.

In child abuse cases, eliciting and maintaining parents' motivation to change can be difficult (MacKinnon and James 1992a). Abusive parents are said to function at relatively primitive ego levels and use a wide range of defense mechanisms that serve to sabotage any therapeutic effort (Salter et al. 1985). Resistance is characteristic of a rigid and dysfunctional system with low levels of ego differentiation that cannot tolerate threats to its equilibrium (Pardeck 1988). Especially where there is a tendency for family transactional patterns to be replicated from one generation to the next (Friedrich 1990, Steele and Alexander 1981, Will 1983), the patterns are firmly ingrained in behavior that is not easily relinquished.

A therapist needs to believe that it is possible to work within these limitations, and to be willing to establish a working relationship that does not necessarily include trust in the therapist, at least not initially. The therapist has to be exceptionally honest with the clients, and the fact that the therapist may be writing reports that will go to court needs to be addressed with the family from the beginning.

FAMILY THERAPY WITH AN ABUSIVE PARENT

Friedrich (1990) outlined several assumptions that underlie the various interventions when working with sexually abusive families. Although his intent was to describe both incestuous and nonincestuous sexual abuse treatment, these assumptions also apply to families that are physically abusive. Friedrich believes that the therapist must be active and willing to direct the therapy from the beginning. This means that the therapist may have to assume therapy case-management responsibilities and coordinate treatment responses with social services and the legal system. It is important that the therapist believe the victim and does not engage with the offender in his denials. Preferably, the offender, rather than the victim, is removed from the home. According to Friedrich, if reunification is not possible, the decision to keep the family separated must be an option. Within all of these parameters, the therapist may need to work with all persons involved.

This willingness to work with all persons involved implies that the perpetrator also may become your client. The therapist must thoroughly examine his or her reactions to this notion. Furniss (1984) suggests that family therapy with a sexual abuse perpetrator needs to include the achieving of clarification in the following five areas: (1) establishment of the facts and clarification of what has happened to whom, in a nonpersecuting and accepting atmosphere; (2) helping the perpetrator to take sole responsibility for the abusive behavior in the presence of other family members, and taking away from the child any responsibility for the abuse; (3) helping the parents to come to an agreement about the degree of their involvement as partners who are both responsible for their children's care and protection; (4) talking openly if the children have been removed from the home because of the abuse so that the children do not see placement as punishment; (5) making a therapeutic contract that contains agreements about the degree of contact among family members and long-term plans for the family.

In the case of incest, the problems are complex. Although Friedrich (1990) suggests that there is a polarization of the sexual abuse treatment field into two nonoverlapping camps— the victim-advocacy group and the family systems group—an integration of these models is possible. This approach would address the individual and systems issues by reinforcing the parental system, enhancing both adults' abilities to get their emotional needs met more appropriately, while at the same time holding the safety of the victim to be of paramount importance.

In cases of sexual abuse, where the abuse itself may have been pleasurable and emotionally gratifying for the child, the deepest part of the trauma comes from the confused role delineations, boundary violations, and betrayals (A. Freud 1981,

Friedrich 1990, Scharff and Scharff 1994). The child does not know how to relate to others in nonsexualized ways, and the child's perception of appropriate relationships has been colored by experiences that he is not equipped to process on a cognitive or emotional level. Consequently, the family must work on clearer definitions and distinctions between roles, and an establishment of age- and sex-appropriate boundaries. This is a family issue that will involve all members of the system.

FAMILY THERAPY WITH
THE NONOFFENDING PARENT

When the offending parent is not available, perhaps because of a prison sentence, refusal to attend, or because the family has been split, family therapy includes the nonoffending parent and children. It is important to know the spouse's intentions regarding the offending parent. Is a divorce imminent? Is the nonoffending parent emotionally tied to the abuser? Are the parents talking about reunification?

The reason this is important is that for the abused child, the ambiguity can be worse than knowing. Just as in games, children will always do better if they know the rules. Even unfair rules can be adjusted to, and the child then at least has the security of knowing what they are and can respond accordingly. However, if a child does not know the rules, the stress continues and escalates every time he thinks he perceives some indication of what to expect. The child will be constantly alert for clues that will tell him whether or not the offender is coming back. Because abusive families are famous for mixed messages and secrets, addressing the ambiguities as they come up is extremely important.

We cannot assume that because there has been abuse, the child has been traumatized. Often, it is the parent who has been traumatized, not the child. Here again, there may be a need to assess more than just the identified client, as this case involving a 5-year-old boy who had been molested by his grandfather demonstrates.

> The molestation involved only fondling, and the child had told his parents immediately. The parents called the police and wanted to prosecute, so there were many retellings of the story to detectives and prosecutors. Because of the court proceedings, I suspected that therapy was initiated in the hope that I would say how awful this experience had been for the child and how damaged he would be because of it. In actuality, I found the process of prosecution and his mother's overbearing reaction much more traumatizing for him than the actual incident. The boy was clearly mourning the loss of his grandfather, with whom he had had a close relationship. He did not want to testify. The mother disclosed that she had also been sexually abused for many years by this man. Although I was in full support of prosecution, it seemed as if it was the mother who needed therapy for unresolved issues that were being projected onto the child. My recommendation was that we stop focusing on the child's supposed trauma and let him be a 5-year-old again.

The therapist will want to assess the level of attachment each family member feels toward the abuser and how each perceives the abuser now. Generally, it is best to assume that the goal of therapy is not to hate the abuser. A goal of therapy may be for the family to recognize all of the conflicting feelings they have for the abuser. Developmentally, children will tackle this issue differently, depending upon their ability to integrate concepts, but older children and the nonoffending parent can help younger children come to terms with their feelings in simplified versions once the child has the ability to integrate both good and bad into one concept.

The issue that the child or children will have with the non-offending parent is that of protection. Where was this person? Why was he or she not available? Why did this person betray the child and not provide the protection he needed? The following case vignette, from a family introduced in Chapter 3, shows how helping the nonoffending parent take a more active role with the children can be practiced metaphorically within the therapy hour.

A mother and her six children, aged 4 through 12, were seen in family therapy because the father murdered another sibling, a 7-year-old girl. Initially, the children were emotionally tied to their father and could not integrate the concept of the murderer with the concept of their father. Thus, they drew pictures of a happy family, including the father, and pretended that everything would be perfect in the family once the father was out of jail. The mother did not dispute this notion, and her ambivalence about the relationship was clear, which prevented the children from seeing the possibility of a dark side to their father. It became apparent in family art therapy that the mother was understandably depressed, having just lost a child, and consequently had no energy to deal with her children's behavior or feelings. In a family art assessment that included a member of the extended family, it was also obvi-

ous that the mother was a youngest child and was still perceiving herself as a child. When asked to draw her family of
origin, she actually drew herself as an infant. She did not know
how to take on the roles of adult parenting. This was borne
out in the dynamics of the sessions, in which the children
made all the decisions and usually did as they pleased while
mother sat helplessly depressed.

It is likely that the mother went from being the youngest in her family of origin, with no responsibilities or expectations, into a marriage with a domineering man who made
all decisions for the couple. The most immediate goal was
for the mother to begin to take on leadership in the family,
something that she had never done. This was achieved indirectly through family art tasks that were designed to force
her into the role of a leader and decision maker. For example,
I would suggest that the family work on a mural, but asked
the mother to choose and organize the art materials. The
children mightily resisted this notion, but with support the
mother was able to stay with her decisions. Or, I might limit
materials and put the mother in charge of their use. In one
case, when the children were making sculptures, the mother
was asked to operate the glue gun. This required that the
children go to their mother when they needed glue, and required her to assist them, symbolically setting up their dependency and her ability to nurture them.

Art tasks can be structured to meet a tremendous variety
of family treatment goals. As with interpretation of art, there
cannot be a cookbook approach. A therapist will need to individualize the tasks to fit the needs of each family.

WORKING WITH EXTENDED FAMILY MEMBERS

Every child needs to feel a sense of security in his environment. Behavioral changes that are brought about through the course of individual therapy are seldom lasting if the child goes back into a system that requires a different form of behavior or is not supportive of the changes he is making. The therapist may need to search beyond the nuclear family and empower others if the biological parents are not able to take on the positive, supportive roles the child needs.

> Kevin was a 5-year-old child who needed attention, nurturing, and love, and he thrived on getting these things from the therapist. He was scapegoated at home. He did not get new clothes, as did the other children; he was beaten, and he was not fed the same food. He was left at a neighbor's house when the rest of the family went on vacation. Kevin pretended that he did not notice these things, and his defensive approach was to distance himself from others. He detached from family members who caused him stress. I noticed this in my waiting room one day after our session. It was Halloween, so I gave all of my clients that week a treat. Kevin very excitedly ran into the waiting room to show his family. His uncle grabbed the lollipop from Kevin's hand and plopped it directly into his own mouth. Kevin immediately dropped his head and looked sad, and when I asked how he felt about it, he said he felt fine, and he didn't care because he really did not want the lollipop. Not surprisingly, Kevin exhibited behavior problems that seemed to invite abuse.
>
> In art therapy, Kevin had a lot of difficulty with the house symbol (see Figure 8–4). He repeatedly attempted to draw

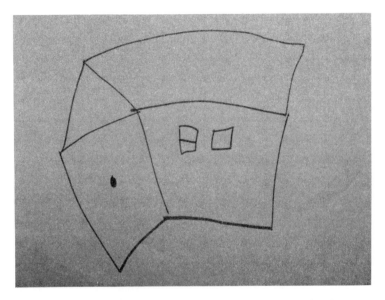

Figure 8–4. Five-year-old Kevin's picture of a house

a house but he was always disappointed with the results. Kevin abandoned these pictures rather than taking them home. Notice how Kevin did not draw a door, and instead there was what almost looked like an umbilical emphasis on the front of the house. His own house betrayed his need for protection and comfort, and hence the house was a difficult symbol for him and one that he was compelled to repeat. Family therapy was attempted but to no avail. Kevin's mother refused to attend after one session. However, Kevin's aunt, who brought him to therapy and was involved in some of the caretaking responsibilities, appeared to be a resource for him. The goals of therapy shifted to involve the aunt in the therapy. Techniques such as time-outs were modeled for the aunt so that she could learn less physical kinds of punishment. I suggested behavioral interventions for her to try at home in the hope that Kevin's acting-out behavior would decrease. Most importantly, she was made aware of the psychological damage being done to Kevin because of the uneven treatment he was receiving compared to his siblings and cousins. She was taught to play some simple games with him that led to positive touch and hugs. One such game involved Kevin sneaking up to his aunt and trying to tickle her. His goal was to tickle and run away. Auntie's goal was to catch him and hug him before he got away. Kevin loved this game, and I suspected it was one of the few times that he was spontaneously hugged. In time, he began to see himself as more a part of the family.

Now, at age 6, as Kevin draws Figure 8–5, it is apparent that the house is becoming a place of comfort for him. Although the house is still not grounded, it is placed within an environment, glitter makes it appear happier, and Kevin is actually pleased with the result, wanting me to hang it in the art room.

FAMILY THERAPY WITH THE FOSTER FAMILY

There are occasions when family therapy with a child and his foster family is warranted, but these occasions are quite specific and need to be clearly boundaried, with goals outlined and defined beforehand. Family therapy with the foster family is a difficult matter purely because of the risk involved in setting up unrealistic expectations for the child. If the child has no parent available to return home to, his dream might be adoption. However, foster families are not always pre-adoptive families. If parental rights have not been terminated, the child may not

Figure 8–5. Six-year-old Kevin's picture of a house

be available for adoption. It may also be that the foster family is not willing to take on the kind of commitment that an adoption requires. Children do not always understand these concepts, and their need to belong and be loved is often much greater than their cognitive ability to understand the legalities of adoption.

However, there are times when the goals of therapy, even intrapersonal goals, require the participation of the persons with whom the child has closest contact. For example, therapists often contact teachers when working on specific behavioral programs for children, so that continuity can heighten the success of treatment. This is also true of the families in which the children live.

If a foster family is included in a child's treatment, it is usually because of specific behavioral goals that are best worked through within the family setting. The therapist must be clear with everyone as to what those goals are. The family must be clear about why they are being asked to come. Most importantly, the child must be clear about why the family is coming. An example of when a therapist may involve the foster family in therapy follows.

Two siblings, aged 4 and 5, were placed in a foster home together after an early history of severe sexual abuse and neglect. The girls were sexually active with one another at every available opportunity. In addition to working with the girls, I worked closely with the foster mother on this behavior and talked to her about setting clear boundaries and reducing opportunities for the acting out. She ceased letting them bathe together and put them in separate bedrooms. However, the behavior continued. The foster mother had a legitimate concern that her 11-year-old son and his friends could become stimulated by this behavior, and felt that the issue was becoming a family problem because she was not always in the room when the behavior occurred and needed help with supervision. A family session was scheduled to talk about this problem. Before the session, I talked to the girls about why the family was coming. "Your foster family really cares about you," I said, "and they want to know ways that they can help you with your touching problem. You and I have worked on this problem, but now we need to figure out what your family can do at home that will help you stop." The foster family, which included six other children and two parents, was initially shy and reluctant to talk about the problem, but by the end of the session everyone was willing to acknowledge how the behavior affected them. For some of the children it was embarrassment, and for others it was "gross." Caring and commitment were also clearly conveyed and the girls seemed very much a part of the family. The family was closely knit and had a natural, teasing rapport, appearing to be well-adjusted as a family unit. They were able to express their feelings in ways that sounded supportive and helpful. Ultimately, the family agreed to a four-part plan: (1) the two girls will never be alone together and all family members will help supervise; (2) the girls will stay in separate bedrooms (already accomplished); (3) the other children in the household will immediately tell mom or dad if they catch the girls in sexual play; and (4) mom or dad will give immediate consequences for sexual behavior, such as separating the children for a short time.

Family therapy may be necessary when a therapist is working with behaviors that are not exhibited within the therapeutic relationship. Involving the family may be the only way to catch the children in the act so that appropriate responses can be made. As long as specific reasons for doing family therapy with a foster family are understood by all, it may be the best option to help the child.

FAMILY THERAPY WITH THE PRE-ADOPTIVE FAMILY

Once a family has made a commitment to a child for adoption, a conscious effort must be made toward achieving appropriate attachment and communication between parent and child (Harvey 1991). The child may continue to have to resolve intrapsychic issues; however, resolution of abuse issues and development of identity become major concerns within the context of a familial relationship. Are there core issues that need to be resolved before interpersonal relationship issues can be resolved, and before the child can accept adoptive placement? And, for a child whose early object relations consisted of rejections and abuse, is formulating a trusting relationship with a new family possible?

Therapeutic strategies can be devised to facilitate the attachment process among adoptive parents and their adopted children. The therapist can set up situations for the family that invite playful interactions. For example, Jernberg's (1979) "Theraplay" techniques, which are based upon the intimacy and physical interplay characteristic of normal, healthy relationships between mother and child, give the family permission to touch and be touched in safe, playful ways. Harvey (1990, 1991) has done some fascinating work with abused children and adoptive families. He suggests that children's movement expressions with adoptive parents have significant expressive phases that are related to past experiences with a birth parent, especially in cases where the child has been abused. For example, the child might produce interactive movement behavior related to passivity, aggression, agitation, sexualization, or direct movement that reenacts the trauma. If this kind of movement is observed while children are interacting with their current parents, it may be a signal that interactive movement memory is operating. The therapeutic goal of an interactive arts approach is to assist families in producing more effective and appropriate expressive intimacy. The wish is for the family to learn new modes of interaction that no longer rely on past influences, but rather are expressive of the new relationship. Harvey's techniques involve movement, drama, and play that allow the family members to experiment with new roles and to respond effectively.

In art therapy, scenarios that require the family to interact can be set up both for assessment and for treatment purposes. Group tasks, such as a family mural or family sculpture, help the therapist understand the family's interactive pattern, and interventions can be made through the art process to facilitate attachment.

I saw Vickie (see Chapter 5) for two years of individual therapy, through two foster homes, one residential treatment center, and a pre-adoptive foster home. Vickie had established a number of rituals through the course of therapy. We always began with a *Highlights* magazine, which she brought into the office from the waiting room. She would sit on my lap and do the Seek-and-Find puzzle in the magazine. Then, we would either play House or Vickie would choose to do an art project. Typically, we would end the session with the Co-Oper Bands. Vickie loved to stretch the band tight and then let go, allowing herself to be propelled into my waiting arms.

One day, Vickie did not bring in a *Highlights* magazine from my waiting room, and did not then sit on my lap and work the Seek-and-Find puzzle. Instead, she proudly walked into my office and handed me a letter from her foster mother, saying that she was going to adopt Vickie. Vickie was quite excited, and immediately began showing signs of change in our relationship. She seemed more independent. She did not seem to need to have physical contact with me. In art, she made a pizza with cheese and pepperoni. At the end of our session, we wrote her foster mother a letter, inviting her to come to a future therapy session.

In the following weeks, Vickie's play with the Bands changed in a subtle way. When we played, she choreographed a new game, pulling away and being pulled back to me, but this time with her back toward me. Several weeks later, Vickie brought her foster mother to therapy for the first time. "This is my new mommy," she said, as she led her foster mother by the hand into my office.

"Why don't you show your new mommy around?" I asked. "You can show her some of the toys that you like to play with. Maybe she can play with the Bands and you today." Vickie gave her foster mother a tour of the art room and playroom, ending with the basket of Bands. Vickie and I showed her mother how we played, and then her foster mother took my place inside the circle. Vickie's play with her foster mother seemed to be an excuse to run into her mother's arms repeatedly. I knew then that once the adoption was finalized, she would be ready to terminate therapy.

Მ 9 ᲛᲗ

"I Want a Mama": Annie's Story

Annie's story illustrates how art and play provide an avenue for the child to experiment with new roles and outcomes. A thematic repetition emerges and continues until the child has mastered a particular concept or feeling that has been causing stress. The child is able to control those aspects that are too frightening and overwhelming. This empowerment is an important part of the curative process inherent in expressive work.

Five-year-old Annie was referred to therapy by the child protective services agency. A number of hotline calls were made while she was in the care of her mother. When she was taken into protective custody, she had been badly beaten on her face and arms. She had a broken collar bone, several broken ribs, and two black eyes. She had also been sexually abused by her mother's male friends. Annie was placed in the home of her father, who brought her to therapy. He was distraught by what had happened to his daughter, and was most concerned about Annie's sexual acting-out behavior. Annie would sit on his lap, as many 5-year-olds do, but would then attempt to touch him inappropriately. He said he told her that is not nice, but he did not know what else he should do. Sometimes she would get very kissy with her dad, and he was uncertain if and when he should set limits.

Annie told me some of what happened to her in our second session. She drew a picture of two men and said that one of them put her in a scalding shower and put soap in her mouth, and the other one hurt her "down there," as she pointed sadly to her genital area. I encouraged her to get mad at the picture she drew of the two men (see Figure 9–1), whereupon she defaced it with angry scribbles.

In the third session, she began playing House, which ended up becoming her primary means of expression throughout our work together. In the first weeks of playing House, Annie assigned me the role of mother and herself the role of daughter. She directed me to cook dinner and tuck her in bed. Then she would get up and go to school. This brief scenario would be repeated for approximately thirty minutes. Perplexed about its meaning, one day I asked Annie about the House game, and she said simply, "I like to pretend that I have good parents." We always saved a few minutes of the session to read books about good and bad touch, to play Feeling Charades, or to talk about good feelings and bad feelings.

Annie formed a therapeutic attachment quickly. In the sixth session, she began asking many questions about me, and drew a picture of me. This positive identification coin-

Figure 9–1. Five-year-old Annie's picture of her two perpetrators

cided with play therapy themes that were focused upon the mother tending to her child completely. Her repeated assignment of the good mother role to me suggested that Annie was enthralled with the concept of a good mother.

In the ninth session, Annie remembered more sad things that happened to her, and drew about them. She said her mother told her she was a bad girl and tried to kill her with a knife. "But I wasn't a bad girl," she said sadly. "How do you make a knife?" she asked. "It wasn't pink, but I have to make it pink." Annie was attempting to gain mastery over this traumatic incident by drawing it. Making the knife pink was a way to defuse the feelings in association with the knife. In her House game that week, she continued to choreograph scenes of domestic tranquillity.

About the time of the tenth session, Annie began receiving upsetting phone calls from her mother. Her mother accused Annie of not loving her, and Annie then was forced to tell her mother that she did love her, but did not want to live with her. This was extremely difficult for Annie, and she cried in the retelling of it. The House game changed that week. The daughter got very ill. I, playing the mother, had to carry her to the doctor and then nurse her back to health by taking her temperature, giving her medicine, and feeding her soup. Annie played a pitiful part, feverish and weak. She allowed herself to play the vulnerable, weak person because she trusted that she would be taken care of and nurtured. She wanted to feel this nurturing deeply, and continued this role for several months. Annie was reported to be having nightmares again, coinciding with mother's phone calls.

At the twentieth session, we had to take a therapy break because of a withdrawal of funding from the protective services agency. We had a four-month break in therapy, until the next fiscal year began. It was surprising how much changed over this period of time. Her father reported that Annie's mother was awarded supervised visitation and she was fighting for custody of Annie. Her mother had married Annie's perpetrator, so he was living in her home and would be Annie's new stepfather. Her mother was pressuring Annie to agree to come live with them. In our session, Annie appeared confused and upset. She said that her mother told her the abuse was just in Annie's head. This contradicted all of Annie's own memories, yet she could not reconcile them with the idea that her own mother was calling her a liar. She told me that she thought he did abuse her, and she felt scared when she saw him at her house because she did not want to get beaten up again.

Annie decided to play House in this session, picking up where she had left off four months before. In this game, I was assigned the role of mother, Annie was the daughter, and a baby doll played the baby. Annie's grandmother was in a terrible accident, and Annie called her mother to tell her to go straight to the hospital. When they met at the hospital, Annie told her mother that her grandmother had died. Then, her stepfather called and said that he was going to kill Annie and the baby. Annie said, "If my stepdad kills me, I'll kill him back."

This session represented the considerable turmoil that Annie was feeling. She was terrified of her abuser, was feeling alone and helpless, and was mustering up the courage to provide for her own protection. In her next session, she announced upon her arrival that she was having bad dreams and decided that she wanted to make a book of her dreams. This was Annie's way of regaining control over some of her confused and frightening feelings. I asked her to describe the first dream as she drew it (see Figure 9–2).

"In my dream I'm locked in a cage and I was scared and I feel like I'm dead," she said. "I was scared of [stepfather], you know, that guy that beat me up."

After she drew a smile on the person in the cage, she said, "I can only make happy faces," again indicative of Annie's need to control the situation and her feelings about it. "And this is what the knife looks like."

"Was there a knife in your dream? What did it do?" I asked.

Figure 9–2. Five-year-old Annie's drawing of a bad dream

"Stabbing me. And there was blood in my dream," she said as she scribbled a spot of red underneath the knife. "In my dream, it was [stepfather] with the knife."

When she was finished, I asked Annie if she wanted to draw another dream for her book. She said she was not drawing a book. I reminded her that at first she said she wanted to do a book, which was why we had gotten out the stapler. She responded that she would draw only one more picture and it would be a good dream. Annie had reached the limit of what she could possibly process in one session, and exhibited enough ego strength to end with a more positive feeling. Her final picture was of a friend, and she announced that her book of dreams was complete.

Then Annie wanted to play House. She choreographed a different story this time. It began with Annie as a baby, but she grew up quickly, and then was a little girl helping her mother cook. While the mother was at work, the baby-sitter "child abused" Annie. The mother believed Annie and called the police and the baby-sitter was put in jail. Then, the mother had another baby girl, whom she also named Annie. The older Annie watched the new Annie while her mother was at work, and made the baby a beautiful birthday cake, with all kinds of colors.

This new twist to her House theme indicated Annie's strengths and ability to self-soothe, for Annie is represented by both the child and the baby in the story. The fact that Annie's mother believed her in the story, and the perpetrator went to jail, was Annie's way of experimenting with a new ending to her own story. This story was the beginning of a new thematic repetition in Annie's play therapy. Instead of being sick and needing nurturing, Annie was beginning to try on the role of the nurturer herself. Annie needed this role, as she was being placed in some extremely stressful situations and needed to learn to cope with them.

In the next session, Annie struggled with the mixed messages she was getting from her mother. On the one hand, her mother was bribing her to come live with them by promising Annie new toys and clothes. On the other hand, Annie received another letter from her mother denying that any abuse took place, and pretending that they all could live happily ever after. Annie brought the letter to therapy, and when I asked her what she thought of the letter, she replied, "Disgusting. I am mad at my mom 'cause she let people hurted [sic] me." We talked about confusing feelings, and how you can feel two different ways at the exact same time. We talked about which of her parents she might want to live with. I asked about her stepfather, and whether or not he would be at her mother's house if she lived there. "I'd go to my room whenever he comes home from work. I guess I don't want to live with my mama 'cause I'll break my dad's heart . . . he'd be sad. But I miss my mom . . . my mom is going to buy me clothes and toys if I live with her. She already got me a dog and cat and I don't want to lose them. . . . Are you married? Could I live with you and you could be my mama? I want a mama . . ."

In her play therapy, again Annie assigned herself the role of an older child; the doll was the baby, and I was the mother. In this story, Annie made a cake for a surprise party for her mom, who was going to Hawaii for fifty-two weeks. Once in Hawaii, the mother called home, and Annie sounded sad on the phone so the mother figured out something must be wrong. The mother called the police to check on Annie and the baby. The police discovered that the baby had died. Annie called her mother on the phone to tell her, but then announced proudly that her mother was not to worry, because Annie was going to have a baby! She named the new baby Gussie.

The next week, I made a hotline call on Annie's behalf. Although she had not divulged any current abuse, I believed that her visits with her mother were not being supervised and included the stepfather, which was forbidden by the court order due to the past abuse. Ultimately, the case went back to court, and Annie's mother lost her quest for custody. Once her father had undisputed custody and the child protective services agency withdrew from the case, we had to terminate our therapy. In Annie's last few sessions she symbolically communicated what our work had meant to her. She drew a picture of the two of us, with "love" written on both of our faces. When we played House, Annie required that I, playing the mother, be the sick one. Annie tended to me, brought me medicine, covered me up. "I take care of you like you take care of me!" she announced. In art, she made a cemetery out of tissue paper and glue. "I'm making a cemetery . . . for someone who I have been coming to see for a long time," she said, symbolically mourning the termination of our relationship.

In our last session, we drew pictures for each other. In her final House story, Annie had me play a mother who found an abandoned little girl (played by Annie) on her doorstep. The mother brought her inside and fed her. The mother called family services and they told the mother she could keep the little girl! Needless to say, this session ended with Annie's tears.

The complexities of Annie's symbols can be read a number of ways. In her stories, her mother was the idealized mother. This mother was all-good and nurturing. At first, Annie choreographed the stories so that she received good mothering and nurturing from the therapist. She was sick, and the mother tended to her completely. Gradually, the story changed. As Annie became emotionally stronger, she was able to take on some of the nurturing herself. She tried on this role tentatively at first, and developed it further in each session. Although her life situation continued to cause her emotional stress and turmoil, Annie was beginning to learn to control those parts that she could control. For example, she made a frightening knife pink, and she drew herself in the cage smiling. This was not denial, for Annie knew the emotion she was drawing. This was her way of finding a way to control her stress, and it signified growth.

Annie mourned the end of our relationship, and symbolically depicted this in her art. Her metaphor allowed her the opportunity to identify her feelings of sadness. She occasionally fantasized that I would be her mother, yet we also talked about the reality of this whenever it came up. I could not be her mother, but I was able to help her through a very difficult time in her life by providing an avenue of safety for her to explore overwhelmingly difficult feelings.

◖◗ 10 ◖◗

"I'll Live with My Mom When She Gets Her Life Together":
Tammy's Story

One of the important aspects of working with children in foster care is the often temporary nature of the placements. In three years of work with Tammy, she was in three different foster homes, one residential treatment center, four daycare centers, and had a succession of three social workers. The therapist was the only consistent person in her life. This is one of the reasons therapy for children in foster care must be long-term. The therapist may be the only thread of continuity the child knows.

Tammy's story demonstrates how, through long-term therapy, a child's themes change in relation to stressful events in her life. Her story has been subdivided according to changes in her living situation to demonstrate how, with each significant change, Tammy's play and art also changed. Through her themes, one can see how she coped with stress. Ultimately, she found the curative path through her art and resolved her dilemma of separating from her mother and attaching to her foster family. This could not have been choreographed by the therapist. Rather, the therapist had to follow Tammy's lead, trusting the process.

Tammy was placed in foster care when she was 4 years old. She was the only child of a 19-year-old drug addict. The court intervened when her mother left Tammy in the care of others for days at a time, and the mother was reported to the child abuse hotline for medical and physical neglect. Tammy was placed in a foster home and the court set up weekly supervised visits between mother and daughter. The mother's whereabouts were usually unknown, although she showed up for visits when she was not using drugs, usually no more often than once every few months. Once placed under protection of the court, Tammy had a succession of three unsuccessful foster home placements because of her sexual and aggressive acting-out behavior with other children. Psychological testing prior to my seeing her suggested that Tammy may have had higher potential than her high Borderline scores on WPPSI-R (Wechsler Pre-School and Primary Scale of Intelligence-Revised) indicated, and her significant deficits and delays were likely to be reflections of her early lack of cognitive stimulation as well as her depression. Tammy was diagnosed with Adjustment Disorder with Depressed Mood and Reactive Attachment Disorder (American Psychiatric Assocation 1994).

TAMMY LIVING IN A FOSTER HOME:
FIRST FIVE MONTHS OF THERAPY

I began seeing Tammy when she was 5 years old, when she was in her third foster home within a year. Tammy was reported to be very guarded, distrustful, and anxious in most situations, rarely laughing or playing spontaneously. She was noted to seem depressed much of the time, crying for no apparent reason both at home and at daycare. She appeared unable to attach to her foster mother.

Tammy's initial therapy sessions were fraught with anxiety. When she came into the sessions, she hid under the table, sucked her thumb, and silently cried. She would neither talk nor look at me. I allowed her to control the physical distance of our interactions. I offered her choices of art materials by laying them on the table and describing them. Slowly she would emerge from under the table and accept the materials. When she drew, her developmental delays became obvious, as evidenced by Figure 10–1, one of the first drawings she produced in therapy. Her drawings were at a 3-year-old level. She was beginning to make crude figures and was experimenting with combining shapes. Tammy did not engage in spontaneous play and did not explore the art room with any excitement, as other children do. Yet, at the end of our first few sessions, Tammy cried because she did not want to leave.

After several weeks, Tammy began to feel more comfortable in the therapy room. Only then did I feel she was ready for a drawing assessment. I asked Tammy to do a series of specific drawings so that I might evaluate her cognitive and emotional adjustment. Her first picture was a free choice, and she drew: "Keisha. She a girl. She got all the candy." As she was drawing, she began talking. "I don't live with my mom. She was on drugs." I asked what kind of drugs her mother was on, trying to assess her understanding. "White. She had dope too. I'll live with my mom when I get out of

**Figure 10–1. Drawing by Tammy,
a 5-year-old female**

foster care." I asked what else happened when she lived with her mom. She answered, "That man started pushing my booty. Then he took our clothes down. Then he took our clothes off. Then he was sticking his dick in my mom's booty and mine. She hit him and cut his neck off. That wasn't our daddy, it was our uncle."

Next, I asked her to draw her family. "I'm not drawing our uncle. He the one I talked about." Her concept of family included her aunt, two cousins, and herself. For the next drawing, I asked her to draw her mother. She did so, and then drew four more cousins.

Drawing made it safe for her to start talking. When children draw, it seems to circumvent their usual defenses, and in explaining their pictures they often spontaneously reveal things they would never talk about if one asked them directly. It is safer to talk about a picture than it is one's own feelings. Tammy told me much more than I anticipated. In later sessions, if I asked her questions directly, she would not answer. But if I just listened as she drew, she often volunteered her perceptions of her earlier life. She talked about going to drug houses and being left there for a long time. She remembered white drugs.

Tammy tentatively tried out the Co-Oper Bands. Although there are many ways they can be used with groups and individuals, I find it useful in allowing a child the opportunity to experiment with closeness and distance. We both get inside of the circle, which is about five feet in diameter, with the band at our waists. I plant myself relatively rigidly, and let the child test pulling back and coming toward me. The tension of the band gets greater the farther the child pulls on it. Sometimes children exert all of their energy in pulling away, and never come toward me at all. Then I have to follow them around the room. Some children tentatively pull out and carefully control how far they move toward me. More secure children experiment until they discover that they can pull away far, and then if they let go they can be propelled into my waiting arms. I always let the child make up the games and choose which ones we play. The child should control if and when touch occurs. It is interesting to see how a child's play with the Bands changes throughout treatment.

Tammy's initial Band play indicated that she was awkward with touching. She did not know how to reach out. She was afraid of the tendency for the Band to propel her toward me after she pulled away, and always stopped herself about three feet short of touching me. Yet the Band helped her to use touch for soothing later, in a more controlled situation. At the end of that session, she initiated sitting on my lap.

As Tammy became more comfortable with me, she explored the art room further. She found the anatomical dolls, and I assessed her understanding of names for body parts. She played kinesthetically in the sandtray, never developing a story, but seeming to enjoy the tactile quality and the sensation of pouring sand. She usually ended our sessions by having me read to her, which allowed her an opportunity to sit close to me on the pillows or on my lap.

During this period of therapy, Tammy's social worker reported that Tammy was initiating sexual play with other children in her daycare. When a child is acting out sexually, the potential for the child to be a repeated victim with older children as well as a perpetrator with younger children necessitates a direct approach. The behavior must stop. Therefore, I talked to her foster family about consequences, and talked to Tammy directly about her behavior each time an incident was reported. We read books, and we talked about the difference between good and bad touch. Tammy thought everything—good touches and bad—was nasty. We also worked on identification of simple feelings through playing Feelings Charades.

TAMMY MOVES TO A RESIDENTIAL TREATMENT CENTER, AND MOTHER'S VISITS CEASE: MONTHS SIX TO EIGHT OF TREATMENT

After five months of therapy, Tammy was removed from her foster home. It had been reported that her foster mother was hitting her with a belt. Her foster mother requested her removal because of her behavior, and she was placed in a residential treatment center.

By this time in her treatment, Tammy had begun to bond with me. She anticipated her sessions, and remembered from one week to another what she had done previously. She took total control of the sessions, and decided in what order we did things. She always included the Co-Oper Bands in her repertoire. Now she felt secure enough to be propelled into my arms, and she seemed to love this physical contact. It allowed her to get hugs without asking for them. One day she said, "You hug me so I don't fall," indicating her reliance on me for external support. She often asked me to read her a story, and sometimes chose a book called *Don't Hurt Me, Mama* (Stanek 1983). She seemed to be struggling with understanding her own mother's drug addiction and abusive behavior, although she could not consciously talk about this. She loved a book called *I Like Me!* (Carlson 1988) and had me read it five or six times in a session, suggestive of her budding improved self concept. In her sandplay, she made "flowers" out of colored paper, and planted them in plastic cups with sand. This developed into a ritual of her taking on the job of watering my plants, a job she continued throughout the rest of her therapy. When a child moves from needing nurturance to being able to nurture, a tremendous gain has been made in therapy. Tammy had received nurturing from me, and transferred this to the idea that the plants needed her. She took her job very seriously.

Tammy's mother ceased her visits altogether in the ensuing months. Throughout this time, Tammy got tearful whenever she thought of her mother. She wondered why her mother did not visit. She kept saying she would live with her mom "when she gets her life together." Occasionally, she would fantasize that her mother was going to get her back. "My mama went to a place so she can get me back. Tell the social worker I told you that 'cause my mama already got her life together so she can get me back. I won't be seeing you anymore," Tammy announced, dismissing me. This despair for mother affected her sessions greatly. She became ambivalent about the Bands, often not using them at all in a session. She began to get angry with me for not giving her soda, candy, and toys. She discovered the baby doll during this period of therapy. During one session, she cuddled on my lap as she clutched a baby doll toward herself. She kept saying she was going to take the doll home. I told her she could play with the doll whenever she came to see me, but the doll had to stay in my office. Tammy spent the rest of her session expressing her anger and frustration. She moved from my lap to under the table, back to my lap, to the floor. She wanted to sit on my lap, but became too angry to stay there. She wanted that doll. She finally agreed to find a safe place to keep the doll for the next week. She hid the doll in my inner office, a place where children do not usually go, under a drafting table. She insisted she did not want any other children playing with this doll.

Tammy's neediness and depression led to her constant annoyance with me because I could never fix things just right. When she needed help with a project, and I tried to help, I did everything wrong. I reflected these feelings back to Tammy, saying things like, "It seems like I don't know how to help you today, and it's making you feel more angry." Tammy would not respond to my words.

TAMMY LIVING WITH A NEW FOSTER FAMILY:
MONTHS ELEVEN TO TWENTY-FIVE OF THERAPY

Tammy's behavior changed dramatically the following week, when she came to her session with a new foster family. She announced that her mother "isn't my mom anymore, 'cause I have a new family." She made a flower and "planted" it in sand for her new foster brother. I brought the foster family in at the end of the session, and Tammy "read" one of her favorite books, *I Like Me!* (Carlson 1988), to them. At the end of this session, Tammy put the doll she had been hiding back on the shelf.

Tammy's adjustment to this foster home brought many changes in her therapy. She almost immediately became more affectionate and appeared happier. She began to love the Bands again, and wanted to be propelled into my arms at least ten times before tiring. During one session, as I was jotting down process notes, Tammy asked me to write, "I love you Tammy" and " I want to see you Tammy" in my notes.

Tammy's new foster parents were loving, consistent, and understanding of her needs, and she metaphorically brought them into our sessions. She would call her foster mother on the toy phone to talk. When she made an art project, she always made a duplicate one for her foster brother. I talked to her foster parents on the phone regularly. Her foster mother reported that often Tammy said, "I'm going to live with my mom when she gets her life together." One day she said sadly, "I don't think my mom is going to get her life together."

Tammy's ambivalence about her new relationships played itself out in the foster home in the same ways it did with me. When her foster parents disappointed her or had to set a limit for her, she became sad, and cried inconsolably for her mother. When someone said "no" to Tammy, it was like dissolution of all love in her eyes, and she would become distraught, tearful, and withdrawn. We worked on self-soothing techniques Tammy might employ when she missed her mother too much.

Unexpectedly, in the thirteenth month of therapy and after a three-month hiatus, her mother resurfaced for a visit. Tammy told me about this visit, and said, "She said she off of drugs now. When it's my birthday, she said I get to come home." She did not see her mother at Christmas several weeks later.

In January, Tammy had her sixth birthday, and came into her session so excited! We made hot chocolate together to celebrate. A week after her birthday, Tammy began to deteriorate emotionally again in her sessions, as she realized that her birthday had come and gone and her mother had not come to get her. Her frustration at her mother's inability to meet her needs was played out again in our sessions. She would announce something that she wanted to make in art, but would choose materials that would not work, and then would get frustrated because she could not complete the project. For example, one session she brought in a stuffed animal, and said she wanted to make a swimming pool and a food cart for him. She insisted on making this out of paper, despite my caution that it would not be sturdy, and another material, such as craft sticks, might work better. She wanted to do it her way, without my help, and then when it collapsed, Tammy collapsed, lying in the fetal position on the floor and sucking her thumb. The following week she announced that she wanted to make a house. I reminded her that the previous week she got frustrated because we used paper, and she said we could make it out of craft sticks. She got frustrated again, however, when she saw that the house she was making would not be big enough for her to get inside. Her chosen metaphors of the house, pool, and food cart, and the ultimate failure of these projects, reflected her own frustration at not having a stable home with her mother. She withdrew under the table when these projects failed. She left me feeling as if I had failed her again and again, for not knowing that size was an important criterion when she made her house, for not knowing what she needed, for not being able to help her. Yet I also knew that the frustrations she was experiencing went far beyond the chosen metaphors, and were reflective of deep longings for a mother who could never meet her needs.

Throughout this period, Tammy was extremely unsettled about attaching to her foster family. She was petrified about attachment, and the closer she got to her foster parents, the more she struggled. In spite of this, she found herself loving the attention they bestowed upon her. She made sculptural pieces out of found objects for herself and her foster brother, becoming more involved in the art process, experimenting with "special" materials such as reflective paper and glitter. She more or less ceased her play with the Bands, indicating less reliance on me for nurturing as those needs were being met at home. In her sandtray play, Tammy began repeating themes of animals trying to get home, suggestive of her own dilemma of still wanting to go home with her mother.

She continued to have tearful sessions when she was thinking about her mother. At these times, I could never possibly meet her needs, and when she would get frustrated with me I would tell her that I was sorry that she was feeling so sad, and I wondered if she was missing her mother. I told her it did not seem I would be able to fix things so that she would feel better. I tried to help her identify these feelings so that when she missed her mother at home she could tell someone, and receive additional nurturing. During this period of therapy, Tammy also began expressing her wish for a sister.

TAMMY'S FOSTER FAMILY WORKS TOWARD ADOPTION: MONTHS TWENTY-SIX TO THIRTY-SIX OF THERAPY

The court was getting very frustrated with Tammy's mother's inconsistent visitation (she had seen Tammy only once in the previous year), her repeated jail convictions, and her refusal to complete drug treatment, so termination of parental rights was initiated as we were beginning our second year of therapy. Tammy's foster family adored Tammy and wanted to adopt her. Her foster mother told her this one weekend, and the next session I asked Tammy if she had any news. "Who did you talk to?" she asked. I told her. "I want my mama," she answered, as a huge tear formed at the corner of her eye. Tammy said she did not want to get adopted because her mother was going to get off drugs. She did not want to talk about adoption, and every time I mentioned the word, she clouded up and her bottom lip extended out in a huge pout.

Tammy's mother was in jail for an extended period of time, so there was no contact with her. Tammy continued to be sad but hopeful, and said that her mother would come to get her when she was out of jail. She made many projects for her mother, and wrote "I love you mom," on them, but would invariably give the projects to her foster mother, signifying her security in her foster mother's love for her. One evening when she was feeling particularly sad, she asked her foster mother if she was still going to be adopted, and Tammy said she did not want to be. The next day, Tammy got into a fight on the school bus, and scratched another child in anger with a rusty nail. Tammy did not know what to do with her frustration. She refused to talk about this in therapy the next day. However, she made and wrapped presents for each member of her foster family, as if symbolically apologizing. She said when everyone got home that evening, they would pretend it was Christmas.

During this period of therapy, Tammy revisited the issue of her own sexual abuse, an issue that had not come up for over a year. She found a book, *Sarah* (Katz 1994), and asked me to read it. The book is about an 8-year-old girl who gets sexually abused by an uncle while her parents are at work. The next three weeks she chose the same book, making no comment. At the fourth week, Tammy said that what happened to Sarah happened to her, and that her uncle said the same thing as the uncle in the story, that he would hurt her mother if she told. By rereading this story over and over again, Tammy was trying to understand her own feelings. There were some weeks that she asked me to read the story four and five times within a session. At this age, through her identification with the character in the book, she was able to understand that it was not her fault. We read this book weekly for eight weeks.

When Tammy's mother got out of jail, visits were set up once again. This made Tammy's confusion all the more pronounced, for to her it meant her mother was getting her life together, and hence, how could she be adopted?

When Tammy's mother failed to show up for visits, Tammy again began getting frustrated with me and again set up art-making situations that were destined to fail. For example, Tammy said that she wanted to make a pair of shorts. My own sewing abilities are quite limited, and I felt that she had finally pushed me to the brink of my talents. I told her I could not help her make a pair of shorts, but I knew that her foster grandmother sewed, and perhaps she could help Tammy with this project. Tammy fell apart, for once again, in her eyes, I was rejecting her; I was not able to meet her needs; I was useless. "It sounds like you are really missing your mom right now," I said. Tammy cried, and sat in my lap and sucked her thumb while I rocked her.

During this period, Tammy mentioned wanting to make a "sister" again. It was at the end of a session, so we did not have time to do this. Instead, we picked out some boxes that looked like they'd make a good head and body, and reserved them for her for next time. The next session, she no longer had an interest in making her sister. However, four months later, Tammy was ready to make a "sister." I had no idea what the significance of the sister might be but knew that this theme had been hovering for a long time, and it seemed that finally Tammy was ready to approach it.

We retrieved the boxes we had saved and gathered doll hair, Styrofoam and cardboard. The sister (see Figure 10–2) took two weeks to complete, which was significant for Tammy, as she had never previously been able to delay gratification that long. When she took the sister home, the importance of

Figure 10–2. Six-year-old Tammy's sculpture of her "sister"

the project was revealed. She named her sister Tina, and Tina took on the roles that Tammy could not, for fear of betraying her own mother. Tina asked to sleep with the foster parents. Tina watched the foster mother work on the computer and cook dinner. Tina told the foster mother that she loved her.

The object relations issues were too complex for this child to possibly articulate. She could not betray her own mother by loving her foster parents, although she did love them. She was able to work toward some resolution of this dilemma through her art making. She created herself—a self who could be affectionate without betraying, a self who could express feelings that were too difficult for her to consciously acknowledge, a self who could say and do the things that she could not. This allowed Tammy a "practicing" period, an opportunity to try on a different role, and to see what it felt like to be a full member of a family.

TERMINATION OF TAMMY'S THERAPY

Tammy continually amazed me with her ability to use art to process her feelings. She came into therapy one day and asked if I had a coffee can. As was often the case, I did not know her plan, but she clearly had a mission she wanted to accomplish. She found a coffee can in my junk box and began cutting tiny little pieces of paper, about a sixteenth-inch square, and dropping them into the can. I watched her for awhile, fascinated by her look of determination, and then asked her what she was making.

"Ashes," she announced, as if this were the most natural thing in the world. "You know how when people die, they have something with ashes? That's what I want to make."

"Whose ashes?" I asked.

"My mom's." She then asked me to help her cut up ashes, which I did. She said that she cried about her mom recently, because she still misses her. We talked then about adoption and she said she was ready to be adopted.

When she was nearly satisfied with the amount of ashes in the can, she instructed me to continue the cutting-up process while she took on the important task of decorating the can with pink and blue hearts and stars. Tammy was pleased with her project. She took the can home and kept it on her dresser in her room.

Tammy's mother had not died, but this was Tammy's way of conceptualizing the letting-go process that was necessary in order for her to move on with her own life. Through this art piece, Tammy symbolically mourned the loss of her mother. It seemed to signal that she was finally ready to accept adoption by her foster family.

It was also a signal to me that she would soon be ready to begin terminating therapy, as she was more ready to be part of a family now, and could use her adoptive parents for the nurturing and support that she once had gotten from me. Her foster parents and I talked at length about this, and they felt that she was ready to be "just a normal 8-year-old." When her adoptive mother and I first talked about termination with her a month later, Tammy felt sad. We talked about terminating therapy using the metaphor of graduating, and that it was a good thing. Shortly after this conversation, Tammy decided to make a baby doll out of papier mâché and cloth, a project that we knew would take a number of weeks to complete. Tammy decided that when she finished making the baby doll, we would end therapy. In this way,

Tammy was able to control when termination happened, and made a transitional object to take with her.

At each crucial moment in therapy, Tammy seemed to know somehow what she needed to make. This was not something I could choreograph. With Tammy, I provided the materials, the holding environment, and the safe and trusting relationship that allowed her to try. Tammy found her own path.

The creative process, because it is an unconscious projection, allows the child the opportunity to explore feelings that could not be acknowledged on a conscious, verbal level. Often, we see children find the reparative path in their art-making and play. They cannot follow the path of another child, and the therapist cannot expect that what worked with one child will work with another. Each child has to find his own way of expressing what is deep inside. Each child finds his own path.

❦ 11 ❧

"Art Has Truth":
John's Story

Inscribed in stone high above one of the entrances to the St. Louis Art Museum are the words: "ART STILL HAS TRUTH. TAKE REFUGE THERE." John's story illustrates how one learns to trust the art more than what the child says. Children learn early how to hide their feelings behind words. They do not know how to hide feelings in art, however, and hence when the art does not match what the child says, the art is often a better indicator of what the child is truly feeling. John's story also demonstrates how a child can use art for solace and strength. John was 8 years old when he came to therapy for the first time, and he came to therapy intermittently for the next four years. John's art often reflected feelings that he was denying. Periodically, we reviewed the pictures he drew in art therapy. Through his pictures, we found truth.

John's positive relationship with his mother, who was loving, psychologically stable, and able to follow through on therapeutic suggestions with consistency, made continuous therapy unnecessary. I could see John for short-term intervals, we would address the primary issues at hand, and then he would leave therapy and practice the gains made in therapy with the support of his mother, independent from me. At times of crisis, he came back for a few sessions to re-work some of his issues at an increased level of understanding.

John was the identified scapegoat in a family of five children. His father was an alcoholic, and he criticized John about his appearance and stupidity, although John was an attractive and bright boy. His father was controlling, manipulative, needy himself, and had a violent temper. John's parents' imminent divorce was causing considerable stress in the home. His mother was also in counseling, and attempted to contain the children's anxiety while searching for a new home and balancing a full-time job.

John was completely dominated by his older brother, age 12, who had formed an alliance with his father and mimicked his father's abusive ways toward John. John's three sisters were much younger, and were spared from the abuse because the father and brother had little relationship with them. John's problems were exacerbated by the fact that he was small for his age, underweight, fearful, and insecure. He was not good at sports, as was his brother, and was beginning to withdraw from neighborhood games because he could not keep up. He spent an inordinate amount of time watching television, seeming to find the drama of old movies preferable to his own life. He lied and fabricated stories both at home and at school, even when the truth was a better option.

John loved art, reading, and singing, and his mother thought art therapy might be an avenue for him to express his feelings. Because she could not always be there to protect him, she also hoped that through therapy John could learn how to cope and protect himself from his brother's and father's verbal attacks.

In his first therapy session, John brought in a drawing (see Figure 11–1) to show me, a variation on a theme that he was to repeat many times in the course of our work. This mansion is large, with many windows that are actually too small for the building, tiny doors, and no embellishments that might give a feeling of life within. Undefined turmoil is scribbled into the sky, suggestive of generalized anxiety. There is an overall feeling of depression in this picture. It suggests psychological inaccessibility, loneliness, and a need to withdraw. John drew many such mansions. He drew them in his room when he needed to withdraw from the turmoil in his own home.

Figure 11–1. Eight-year-old John's picture of a mansion

Each week he brought several new pictures to show me. Some of them actually looked more like prisons than mansions, as he would forget to draw the cross-panes on the windows, and they would end up looking like bars.

In therapy, John most often preferred to have me give him some kind of an art directive, followed by free play time. At the end of each session, he brought his mother in to show her what he had done. We began by making a book of feelings. John seemed to have trouble identifying what his feelings were. He had a habit of denying when things were bad and minimized his own feelings of discomfort.

One week, John's mother brought up some concerns that she hoped John and I could talk about. John and his brother were fighting a lot at home, and John had begun taking a knife out of the kitchen drawer and holding it as if he was going to hurt his brother. Although on the one hand John's mother felt that it was positive for John to be standing up to his brother and expressing his anger directly, it was obviously a completely inappropriate and potentially dangerous way to express anger. It unfortunately always happened while she was at work, so she could not intervene on John's behalf.

The first thing John did was to make a picture for his feelings book. He drew a picture titled, *When My Brother Slams Me, I Feel Mad.* John reported that when his mother was not around, his brother would run toward him and slam into him. John drew himself holding the knife. We talked about how the knife did not appear to be causing his brother to stop slamming him, and that it was dangerous and not a good way to deal with the situation. We then decided to think of some things that John could do when his brother slams him that would be more helpful. John came up with a list: "Fight back; go into my room and shut the door; tell mom; use my imagination like Calvin in *Calvin and Hobbes*" (a comic strip). We decided that it would be fun for John to use his imagination and draw a comic about himself and his brother with a different ending, a totally imaginary ending that would help him feel like he had power over the situation. John drew a two-panel cartoon. In the first panel, his brother "pows" him, and he is upset, while his brother smiles and gets ready to slug him again. In the second panel, John turns his brother into a frog. He seemed to enjoy the humor and sense of empowerment he got from drawing this picture. I gave him paper and some homework to do. I told him that I wanted to see another comic next week, and the next time his brother slammed him, he was to go into his room and use his imagination to come up with a comic. The next week, John brought in a cartoon that he did when his brother was bothering him. The picture shows John holding a large magic wand and turning his brother into a tiny mouse. His mother said that it worked well for him. His brother could not figure out what John was doing and ended up not bothering him anymore. When John did a sandtray picture later in this session, he made himself a crocodile and his brother a goldfish and put the goldfish in the crocodile's mouth.

John's work with his feelings about his brother paved the way for him to approach his feelings about his father, who was much more emotionally abusive with him. John spent the remaining sessions putting many complicated feelings onto paper, including his feelings about the "good and the bad" father, his own attempts to get in the middle of his parents' fights, and bad days when his father hit him.

We agreed to a therapy break shortly after John's father moved out of the house. John seemed more able to understand his own feelings, and was able to take a more appropriately assertive role with his brother.

The next time I saw John was a year later. His mother was concerned that he had drifted into the illusion that daddy really loved him and might come back. John would cry that he missed "poor daddy," and seemed to feel abandoned and left out. His father was inconsistent with visitation, and had seen the children only four times during the entire year. We began this session by reviewing his portfolio, which he had left with me for safekeeping. We looked at all the drawings he had made previously in therapy, including his book of feelings. Most were about his father, his temper, his rage, and John's fear and nervousness around him. John filled me in on what had happened since I had last seen him, at first reflecting complete denial. "Things are better now," he said. "I've been seeing him a lot more lately and it's been fine." I asked questions about a few stressful incidents I knew of, and John's defenses broke down. He started talking about lies and disappointments. He drew *How My Dad Acts* and *How My Dad Really Is*. The first was a smiling father at a restaurant with his children. The second was a huge screaming head. After this picture, sensing that there was much more to be expressed, I gave John large mural paper. He scribbled colors and words. He started talking about all of the ways his father had disappointed him over the year, and he made a two-page list of lies, disappointments, selfish acts, and hurts. At the end of this session, we talked with his mother about things John could do, such as quit calling his dad on the phone, and not going with his dad when he is drunk. This "reality check" session helped John pull out of the state of denial where he had been stuck. The drawings served as a reminder to him of his own deeper, genuine feelings. Once he saw his drawings, they reactivated an emotion similar to what he felt when they were created.

I saw John only three times that year. Each time, it was precipitated by a pending weekend visit with his father that had thrown him into a turmoil. Although our refresher visits seemed to help for the crisis at hand, John never seemed able to carry his feelings over from one situation to the next. Each time his father invited him to come to visit, John fantasized that *this* time things would be different. Usually, he would go on the visit, only to call his mother after a day and beg her to come get him.

This pattern continued for the next two years. Although visits were always a disaster, his father somehow always convinced John that it was his fault, and hence John always approached the next visit with the fantasy that this time he would do everything right and his father would love him. John came to therapy the following year preceding a long-weekend trip to a resort lake. He wanted very badly to go on this fishing trip, although his mother pointed out that each time during the past year he returned from visits in tears. John did not want to hear it. In our session, as preparation for his trip, he drew another fantasy (see Figure 11-2). He drew the vacation, a rented van full of people, and John outside the van turning his brother, his father, and his father's friend into frogs. John revisited a fantasy theme that had worked for him in the past, and insisted that he could cope on this trip.

Figure 11–2. John's fantasy picture

The trip ended up being a disappointment to John, as his father left in a boat and did not fish with him at all. When his brother grabbed the journal John had been using to record his feelings and gave it to his father, his father pulled John off the couch and hit him. In art therapy a week later, John drew a picture that reflected the stress and anxiety he experienced (see Figure 11–3).

Each time John drew his feelings, it gave us more accumulated "evidence" to refer back to when his denial was reactivated. However, it was not until the following year, when his father moved out of state, that John had the distance he needed to begin to separate and be more objective. He was invited to visit his father at Christmas, and

Figure 11–3. John's fishing trip with his father

again the turmoil began about whether or not he should go. He drew Figure 11–4, a painting of his own home on the left, and a painting of his father's home on the right. His father's house is on fire and it is raining. The anxiety evident in this picture was in sharp contrast to what John had been saying about how he did not think this trip would go badly. When we stopped to look at his picture, I said, "John, I think in your heart you know that your dad will never be a dad to you."

"I don't want to tell myself that. I don't want to believe it," he answered, as he stared at his picture. "But I do know it. I know he'll always be a horrible father and will never change."

Figure 11–4. John's picture of his two houses

John's pictures often reflected the feelings that he was denying. When we reviewed his pictures, he could not deny his feelings because they were unmistakably depicted in a tangible form. Yet, it took him years to accumulate enough of these truths to use the information to change his reaction to his father. Having "evidence" of his own feelings helped tremendously, and required him to revisit deep places in his psyche. Art helped John find the truth.

✺ 12 ✺

"A Hope Rainbow":
Ebony's Story

The colors in my life
Are not exactly right.
It's like a closed door
In the midnight.
But when I let myself feel
The door will heal
And the colors in my life
Will be exactly right.

—Ebony

Ebony was 14 when she wrote this poem. She used writing as her primary means of expression, along with some artwork. Ninety percent of our therapy was accomplished without ever talking. Because words were too difficult, Ebony and I wrote letters.

Ebony's story is not unlike many children who grow up in institutions. She was removed from her mother's home when she was 3, and by the time she was 13 she had lived in four foster homes and five residential treatment centers.

I met Ebony when she was 13 and living in the residential treatment center where I was the art therapist. I worked with her for three years, until she was 16. As is typical of children who grow up in institutions, Ebony became close to, and lost, many people. She always seemed to be the one left behind, as her friends in residential treatment went into foster homes, or returned to their parents. Ebony repeatedly attached herself to one staff member, only to be disappointed when that person moved on in his or her career and left her. Each significant loss triggered a severe behavioral response. Her preadolescent and adolescent years, consequently, were tumultuous, and included four psychiatric hospitalizations and periodic stays in juvenile detention for assault. Yet, her ability to form relationships made her treatable. Despite repeated losses, she continued to allow herself to get close to people.

During the first six months of her stay in this residential treatment center, the primary issues in her treatment plan were behavioral. Ebony tested the rules in her cottage and shouted at staff when they corrected her. She knew how to get the entire cottage of children in an uproar, would use this as a ploy to make staff angry, and then sit back and laugh while they tried to restore order. She would run out of the house when she was in trouble rather than face her consequences. Ebony was frequently suspended from the on-grounds school, working herself up into periods of extreme hyperactivity and violence, to the point of needing to be restrained. Despite all of this, Ebony was well-liked by both staff and peers. She was impossible to ignore, and could make everyone laugh. She sincerely cared about others. She was fiercely loyal to those she considered her friends and was always ready to defend the underdog. She was sensitive about others' feelings, and knew better than any of the other children when she had hurt someone's feelings. She could then say she was sorry and mean it.

Upon our first meeting when she was 13, Ebony made immediate and intense eye contact, as if trying to determine the safety of a new relationship. She began bonding almost immediately, but tested our relationship continuously to see if I would be capable of her version of closeness. Ebony punished those with whom she was close. She was jealous of other children and attempted to interrupt their sessions; she destroyed art materials rather than sharing them; she knocked on my office door repeatedly to get my attention. She would become angry in Open Art studio sessions when too many other children dropped in, and then would pick a fight with someone to divert attention toward herself. She stopped at my office daily after school to check in, to the point that we began incorporating this into her treatment plan. As our relationship developed, she began writing poems and leaving them in my mailbox.

> Gussie nice
> Gussie sweet
> Gussie is very neat
> She have a personality
> That nobody can beat.

After Ebony had been with us for six months, an older resident sexually molested a younger resident at the treatment center, which triggered painful memories for Ebony that she had never disclosed to anyone before. She wrote a letter to me about what happened.

> Well this foster family I was living with, my uncle, had sexual abuse me and I was feeling bad about myself when that happened yesterday, and it brought a lot of feeling back, but I never told on him cause he had threatened me he would do a lot worse so I didn't tell but I was always scared to go around men. But it hurt a lot now that I'm older cause when I was young I didn't understand it and I cry a lot when I think of it so I try to erase it from my mind cause when I think about it I say to myself think about something nice and make me feel good.

When I saw her in therapy the next day, I asked her if she wanted to talk about the letter. Her response was a resounding "No!" Realizing that she could not possibly verbalize about what she had written, nor could she tolerate me talking about it, I wrote her a letter back. Thus began a nonverbal process of therapy that lasted for three years. Ebony left letters in my mailbox daily, and when she came to her weekly scheduled therapy appointment, I would have a letter in response waiting for her. She read the letter in my office. I always asked if she wanted to talk about anything in our letters. Her answer was always "No." Sometimes we typed letters back and forth during her therapy time, taking turns at the typewriter. This provided the distance Ebony needed so that we could communicate about the things that she could not talk about.

In her letters, she was able to put her feelings into words. She struggled with her feelings of guilt, that even though she was only 6 when it happened, perhaps she somehow pro-voked the abuse from her uncle.

> I feel so low when I think about it. Maybe I provoked it. I just can't think of why someone would do something like that without no reason. I really don't remember doing any-thing to provoke him. I wasn't in bed when my foster mom told me to go. Maybe that was a good reason to do some-thing like that. . . . When he said don't tell nobody I even knew more that it was wrong. Why, why, I really don't understand life. Write back. Do you think I provoke it? . . . Do you think I am a bad person for what happened?

Both Ebony and I sensed the importance of the work we were doing. We began dating the letters and organizing them into a folder. This still was not enough for Ebony, and she also kept journals, which she shared with me periodically. In art therapy, Ebony explored the feelings that intruded into her thoughts and dreams.

> I kind of scared to get married cause I never want some-thing like that to happen to me. I still remember every single thing so clearly and I feel disgusting. I feel dirty or not worth anything.

Still not able to talk, she drew pictures of her perpetrator and defaced them (see Figure 12–1). She wrote down feeling words that expressed the depth of her anger and despair.

Ebony's depression was something that she hid well, but she tried to understand it in her letters.

> Lately I been getting really depressed and sad. I don't re-ally know why. . . . I feel so guilty inside I feel everything

Figure 12–1. Ebony's picture of her perpetrator

is my fault, but why do I have to pay for it if I didn't do anything wrong? Why? It makes me mad Gussie. I shouldn't have to pay for another's mistake! I know the past is overwith but I have to go back and deal with what happened.

She found that red and black were a good combination of colors to express the rage that she felt inside (see Figure 12–2). Hearts, which are a common symbol for children and adolescents, appeared painful when drawn by Ebony.

She would not talk about her images, and I do not often interpret pictures for clients. However occasionally, because

Figure 12–2. Ebony's feelings picture

she could not talk directly, I wrote her what I hoped would
be an empathic response to her imagery:

> You know I looked at the picture you made last night, and
> even though we didn't get to talk about it, I wanted you
> to know that I think it was very expressive. I don't often
> tell you what I see in your pictures, but this one seemed
> really important to me. To me, it seems to represent a little
> of how you've been feeling. The black all around might
> be some depression, but then it opens up into a beautiful
> patch of color. The blue could be You. The red and the
> black seem to be the pain of your past. But the blue is
> graceful and beautiful. It touches the yellow and pink,

reaching out to people, touching their lives. I know that's a lot to see in one drawing, but I believe in drawings, and I believe in you.

As Ebony experienced her anger and shame, and became more aware of the intense anger she felt toward her perpetrator, she wrote him a rageful letter, which she never mailed, about how it affected her life. Although she wanted to scream and punch at pillows in my office, this was something that never worked for her when she attempted it.

I am mad cause I have all these feelings inside and I can't bring them out. It's like I will let myself feel so much anger and hurt and that's it. I'm scared of what might happen if I go down and find out how I really feel. God only knows what might happen. It's like I'm protecting myself.

Ebony began to feel more vulnerable with me because of her disclosures, and was becoming more dependent upon me, both of which were issues that had to be addressed in therapy. She began to use our relationship to get out of dealing with other problems. For example, when she was in trouble in her cottage for not doing chores, she would scream that she had to talk to me, and would work herself into a mad frenzy, sometimes running out of the house and ending up getting more consequences for inappropriate behavior, when all she really needed to do was complete her chore. The houseparents and I met with Ebony together to confront her on this problem, and I followed it up in a letter to her. Her reaction to this was to feel rejected and hurt.

I don't know if I should be writing you this letter cause every time I get in a relationship with someone it gets fucked up.

I just don't want to care and it scares me to hear myself say that, and makes me angry to hear you say I was using you. I have been having a relationship with you and I don't get off on people saying I'm fucking them over!

This was the first time Ebony ever allowed herself to be angry with me, and I wrote her back so that we could talk more about it. Several letters later, her anger subsided. She learned that she could be angry with me, and it did not cause dissolution of our relationship. Unfortunately, Ebony had several immediate losses after this incident. All three of her house parents gave letters of resignation. Because of her attachment to one of them, and her fear of change, Ebony's behavior deteriorated to the point that she was put on a level system all her own, designed for much younger children. She began doing drugs. She smoked marijuana and took any pill that she could find on the streets or at school. I never ask an adolescent a question that I think will result in a lie, so I never asked her directly, but she admitted everything in her letters anyway. She began having indiscriminate sex, and then feeling bad about herself afterwards.

Why do I have sex with guys that I don't care about and they don't care about me, and I go for guys that abuse me? I really want to change this cause this is something I hate about myself and makes me feel bad inside and I guess if I really want to change I have to start with the heart of my problem and that is why do I like doing something that makes me feel bad?

As she wrote about her dark feelings, she continued to feel more vulnerable and more attached to me, and continued to struggle against those feelings. Her fear of being hurt was constant, so each of my vacation days was perceived as a rejection. When I scheduled a week-long vacation, she had to be hospitalized for suicidal gestures. She articulated her fears in poetry, sent to me through a letter.

> They say they're here,
> They say they will stay,
> But then they float away.
> They say they love you,
> They say they care,
> But when you look
> There is no one there.
> I'm scared to trust and let them near
> And tell the secret and my fears.
> They say they love you,
> They say they care,
> But one winter night
> They are not there.

As the relationship issues became more prominent, Ebony decided that she was going to leave the treatment center and began a campaign with her social worker to find her a new placement. The questions that she asked in her letters were complex, and seemed to articulate the deepest part of her problems, which were not related to the physical part of the abuse, but rather to the betrayal of relationships.

I want to ask you some questions. This will help in more ways than one, and sometimes I think you know me better than myself.

1. Why do relationships end up bad for me?
2. Why do I keep building up relationships when I have problems?
3. Why can't I keep a relationship with a boy and I go for guys that don't treat me right or we use each other?
4. How (why) can I care for others more than myself?

My written answers touched on her dependency issues, how she was so dependent upon me that she could not use other people for support, and how that put impossible expectations on our relationship. Ebony wanted to leave because it was too painful to stay. She cut on her wrists and then wrote me a letter, ashamed of being sent to a psychiatric hospital, not able to understand what made her want to feel pain. At this time, she began talking about her real mother, a figure in her life that had remained absent from our therapy sessions all this time.

> I feel that I care less for myself than I have ever in my life. I was thinking about everything that has made me angry or upset in the last year or two. I thought about you and I, I thought about [perpetrator], I thought about my real parents, I thought about the future, I thought about my foster parents. Everything. Sometimes I really want to die, that is the easy way out, I know. But I can't cope with life. I don't know if I should stay or go cause everybody changing my mind. Sometimes I really want to hurt myself bad to make people pay for hurting me. I didn't deserve none of this. I didn't even ask to be born, I just don't understand. I don't understand why I am in a home. I don't understand the situation with my real mom. I don't understand why I want to hurt myself. I don't understand

why I want to leave. I don't understand why I want to stay. I don't understand how I grew to love you so much. Gussie sometimes it hurt so much and I don't understand why and then I want to hurt myself.

Anticipating Ebony's eventual discharge, we decided to make two books of all of our letters, which numbered in the hundreds. Using three-ring binders and a Xerox machine, we made two copies of everything, and arranged them in chronological order. Ebony hand-painted two original covers for the books, and included a poem in the design:

> The rainbow is God's promise
> Of hope for you and me
> And though the clouds hang heavy
> And the sun we cannot see
> We know above the dark clouds
> That fill the stormy sky
> A Hope Rainbow will come shining through
> When clouds have drifted by.

Ebony did choreograph her own discharge, by running away, but that was not the end of our relationship. She continued to write letters, and continued to process her need to reject others first, before they rejected her.

What I learned from Ebony is the importance of relationship in therapy. Ebony's ability to continue to form relationships, despite years of hurts and losses, was the curative piece of our work together. She and I had to have a genuine relationship, not fake, or she could not have tolerated it. It meant that I had to commit myself to our work. Once she attached, I had to see our work through to completion. That she had to leave me before I left her was part of her pattern, but it was one that we continued to work with after she left.

The work that Ebony did occurred on several levels. The first was the issue of sexual abuse, the reactions to being violated at such a young age, and her need to process it at an increased level of understanding as she got older. She struggled with her feelings of guilt, anger, loss of esteem, and fear. However, the underlying issue, that of trust and relationship, was the key to her deeper problems. The rejection by her own mother at age 3 did not emerge as a therapeutic issue until late in her therapy, and yet it was an important key to understanding her. The betrayal of that initial relationship colored all of her relationships, and was repeated many times in rejections from foster homes. It was that initial rejection that she and I had to work through in our relationship.

Although we have not had a client–therapist relationship for over ten years, I continue to hear from Ebony. She is 26, with a 3-year-old daughter, and has a successful career working with troubled teenagers. She now struggles with these issues at an adult level, with much more insight than she had before. In her last letter, she wrote:

I guess the hardest thing for me is that I always felt like I didn't have any family and I built a wall. I became selfish in a lot of ways because I always had to look out for myself. It is hard for me to share because I think I have to take because it might be gone. I'm learning how to really give back without thinking about myself all the time.

At each developmental life stage, as Ebony attends to the developmental tasks at hand, she approaches her past issues at a new level of understanding. Ebony is a success story, thanks to her ability to attach.

◎ 13 ◎

"Stories to Teach about My Mom": Julie's Story

Four-year-old Julie taught me a tremendous amount about how children use symbolism. She also taught me that a therapist does not necessarily need to interpret symbols for a child. The work the child does through play is powerful enough. Julie knew better than I did what her stories were about and how important they were to her healing.

Julie's history is best told in her own words, which she explained as she drew during our first session:

> "I'm drawing my mom. My mom died. She was so sick and she loved me and my sister so much that she wanted us to go with her. Mom said, "Roll over and we'll play a game." She shot me and she shot my sister and I peeked and saw my mom shoot herself. I felt really sad. Now I'm going to draw my sister. My mom and my sister turned into ashes and now they are in heaven. . . . My mom and sister got shot

by a gun and died and I got shot but I didn't die. I don't understand why Jesus did that. And my sister was only 1. It's very sad. I'm drawing my bed [see Figure 13–1] and that's me and that's my mom. I'm not going to draw the gun because I don't know what it looks like. That's my sister and she got shot."

At the end of this first session, when I told Julie it was time to go, she came to where I was sitting, put her arm and head on my shoulder, and began to cry. I pulled her onto my lap as she began sobbing and clung to me. I promised her she would return the following week, and showed her her name in my appointment book.

Julie was shot seven months before I saw her for the first time in therapy. She showed me the scars, front and back,

Figure 13–1. Four-year-old Julie's picture of her family

from where the bullet had gone through her small body. Her traumatic memory of the murder/suicide, including her own attempted murder by her mother, suggested intrapsychic issues that can hardly be fathomed. I began working with Julie within a framework of individual, object relations-oriented goals related to her primary attachment figure and traumatic memory. Not only was Julie able to tell me what happened, she was also able to articulate her feelings as she struggled with existential questions of such magnitude that I often found myself dumbfounded as to how to respond. At the end of our fifth session, after she played most of the hour, I asked Julie if there was anything else she wanted to talk about.

"Why did God do that? Why did my mom shoot me? Why did my mom shoot my sister in the heart so that she died? Why did my mom shoot herself in the heart so that she died? Why did she shoot me so I didn't die? It doesn't help me to talk about it. I don't understand why God did that. I will see my mom some day when I die."

Julie struggled with these questions, and sometimes she also answered them. Several weeks later, as the session neared its end, I asked if there was anything else she wanted to talk to me about.

"Why did my mom shoot me? This is why I think: my mom was sick in the head and she wanted to go see Jesus but she loved us so much that she wanted us to come with her. Do you think that's it?"

Julie was in foster care, and several relatives were fighting for her custody. She formed a therapeutic attachment with me quickly, which seemed to tie in with her need for nurturance. Julie always chose to use the sandtray, a technique of play therapy based upon Jungian theory. The sandtray consists of a multitude of small figurines that the client manipulates to create a story. Julie's stories were complex for her age and sustained her complete interest for the entire fifty-minute session. In the beginning, her stories seemed to relate to the lack of stability and uncertainty of her living situation. She presented stories of children being stolen by "bad guys" and locked in dungeons. Children were threatened and left to die and even Batman could not save them. In one story the bad guy put the girl on "the cross that Jesus died on and poured poison on her head and told her she will die." Initially, none of Julie's stories had happy endings. They either ended negatively or remained unresolved, reflective of her own unresolved life and feelings of hopelessness.

Another repeated theme related to her feelings of guilt that her sister, and not she, had died. In one story, she chose two baby dolls, the smaller one being "my sister, because she was only 1." She put the smallest baby onto a bridge, and the baby began crying because a dragon was coming to get her. The older sister kicked the dragon and carried the baby away and put her in a bed, covering the bed with the bridge, which she said was to protect her.

In many of Julie's stories, she chose three "pretty girls," who she said were sisters, as the main characters (see Figure 13–2). Monsters and witches tried to steal the sisters and kill them, but the sisters always won in the end. Usually one sister was the strongest and saved them all. The sisters found a baby orphan and took her home and took care of her. The sisters saved baby animals. As a team, the sisters appeared invincible.

Figure 13–2. Four-year-old Julie's sandtray picture

The sisters seemed to represent the split-off parts of herself. She was working through feelings about her own mother (represented by witches or monsters in the story) who tried to kill the sisters. One sister saved them, which was the strong part of herself. She expressed guilt about her real sister dying: the repetition of finding a baby orphan and saving her was a means of reworking her helplessness over her sister's actual death. Still, Julie ended each session by asking questions about why her mom shot her. She had a precociousness and maturity about her that made her seem far wiser than her 4 years.

The play therapy themes were similar each week, suggesting her need for repetition of the traumatic memory. Her ability to rework the trauma and put herself in the powerful position suggested her need for control and her tremendous strengths.

As part of my treatment of Julie, because I would be writing recommendations to the court, I interviewed all of the parties who were vying for her custody. Although he lived in another state and despite the fact that they did not have a relationship prior to the trauma, the biological father was the strongest candidate for Julie's ultimate safety and security. After I saw Julie in ten individual therapy sessions, the court awarded custody to her biological father. The court order required that Julie could not be moved for thirty days, allowing a minimal amount of time for bonding to occur between Julie and father, and termination of our therapy. Sessions were increased to twice a week to accomplish these new goals.

Immediately, I had to change the goals of therapy from intrapsychic to interpersonal to meet the more immediate needs of this child. Julie was entering into a new family system and issues of attachment with her father would need to become paramount if this change was going to be successful. I began including the father in the sessions immediately, hoping to help Julie's bonding process with him before they moved. In addition, our termination, and all of the implications surrounding separation, had to be addressed.

Julie's first session with her father reaffirmed my belief that he had an ability to parent appropriately. He was affectionate with Julie, and although quite nervous about his new commitment, he appeared earnest and caring, although young and inexperienced. If possible in this first session, I needed to get Julie to transfer to her father some of the roles she assigned to me in the play therapy. This proved to be easier than anticipated. As usual, Julie went immediately to the sandtray.

Julie: Dad, I want you to play with me.

Dad: I'm watching you play right now, honey.

Julie: I want you to play with me.

Therapist: You know, you might have to teach your daddy how to play the way you and I play. 'Cause he's never done it before. So you can teach him?

Dad: Yeah, I'm kinda new at this.

Julie: We just play however we want.

Therapist: Right. Usually what happens is Julie will tell you exactly what you have to do, right? You'll tell him who he has to be and what he's supposed to say. And she's very good at that.

Dad: I believe that.

Therapist: So, you want your daddy to play with you today?

Julie: Yeah.

Therapist: Okay. He'll be me. Instead of me playing, he'll play?

Julie: Yeah. But, but, but . . . (sounding distressed) but you guys can both play.

Therapist: We could both play. Sure. We could both play.

Julie: I want both of you to play.

Therapist: Okay. You just tell us what to do.

Thus began the first session with her father. I explained to the father that he could not add anything of his own to the plot, but should wait until Julie made all decisions about the story. She truly was good at this, and would tell us both exactly what our characters were supposed to say and do so that the entire story was of her own design and all characters were her own projections.

This story involved the three sisters. A mom alligator who was mean had a baby alligator who was nice. The mom alligator chased the sisters and tried to bite them. However, a new plot twist came into play in this story. The sisters called for Prince Eric (a new fantasy male figure, played by her father) to save them. This introduction of an age-appropriate oedipal relationship and rescue scene was seen as a positive first step. Later in that story, a bad shark began to bite one of the sisters. Again, Prince Eric was the savior.

Julie: I'm pretending that the shark followed her, all right?
Dad: So what does he do when he gets there?
Julie: He bites her.
Dad: He bites her? . . . Where does he bite her?
Julie: Right here.'
Dad: Right here? (biting sound)
Julie: AAAAh!
Dad: Bite bite bite bite. Chomp chomp chomp.
Julie: Owww! I'm going to tell Prince Eric. Prince
   Eric? . . . That shark was biting me right on the hand.
Dad: He was biting you on the hand? . . . What do you
   want me to do?
Julie: You should leave him locked up in a cage.
Dad: You want me to leave him locked up in a
   cage? . . . Okay. . . . (He locks him up in the cage.)

At the end of the story, a bad guy set traps for all of the sisters and captured them in cages. Again Julie choreographed it so that Eric, played by her father, saved them.

Therapist: Okay, let's end this story, then.

Julie: That was the end.

Therapist: That's the end? He's gonna go get a drink of water and the girls are still locked up?

Julie: No. Prince Eric frees them all. . . . And they go back to their home. . . . And they live happily ever after.

Therapist: Well, gee that's a good ending for the story today . . .

Julie: Yeah, I picked it 'cause I liked it. . . . Daddy, you're supposed to free them.

Dad: Okay, you're free, you're free, you're free.

Julie: Thank you.

Dad: You're welcome.

This plot twist was repeated several times in subsequent weeks. Julie's relinquishment of some of her power to her father helped her to feel less responsible for protecting herself. If she could yield some of the control to her father, and form an appropriate attachment to him, she would also be better prepared to do some of the intrapsychic work necessary for her healing.

Termination of our work was more difficult. Julie began having trouble cleaning up and ending our sessions.

Julie: I wish I had a little fox like this (holds up a sandtray figure).

Therapist: Really?

Julie: Yeah, but I don't. . . . I wish I could have this one.

Therapist: Well, we want to keep that one here for next time when you come, so you can play.

Julie: Do you have . . . could I have this to borrow?

Therapist: I don't think so. I need to keep all the animals here.

Julie: Why?

Therapist: So that when kids come, they have the animals to play with. Kids like you. You wouldn't want to come here and not have an animal here that you wanted, would you?

Julie: Well, I would bring it back the other day.

Therapist: Well, let's leave it here and you can play with it next time.

Julie: Why?

Therapist: Because we have to leave the animals here.

Dad: We can look around and maybe find some . . . maybe we can make a sandtray of your own.

Therapist: That would be neat.

Dad: And we could collect all kinds of animals and stuff for it.

Julie: (tearfully) I don't care about that.

Therapist: Julie, let's clean up now.

Julie: I'm mad!

Therapist: You're mad? What are you mad about?

Julie: Because I don't have an animal like that fox. (stomps out of the room)

Therapist: Well, why don't you come in here and we'll clean up and while we clean up we'll talk about it.

Julie: No!

Dad: Julie, come on in, hon.

Julie: (tearfully) No! I don't want to do this! And I don't . . . and I want a fox like that but I don't have one. That's what I'm angry about.

Therapist: I think you're angry about a lot of things. Probably. Maybe we should talk about some of the things that you are angry about.

Julie: No!

Therapist: Well, let's start cleaning up.

Julie: I'm too angry.

Therapist: You are too angry to clean up? . . . Well I guess your dad and I will just have to stay in here and keep playing and talking then.

Julie: (still in other room) What did you say?

Therapist: Well, you'll have to come in here if you want to hear what I'm saying. 'Cause right now your dad and I are going to talk. And you can come in with us.

Julie's father asked her again to come back in, and she stomped in. I told her I thought I understood why she wanted the little fox.

Julie: Oh really? Then why?

Therapist: I think maybe you wanted it because you want to take something that represents you and me. I think you've had a good time coming here and you want something to take with you.

Julie: Yeah . . .

Therapist: And you know what? (Julie begins crying) What? You don't want to talk about that?

Julie: No.

Therapist: I'm going to really miss you too.

Julie leaves the room again, and then is persuaded to come back.

Julie: I don't want to talk or anything. I'm just upset.

Therapist: I know you're upset. You know, Julie, I'm a little upset too.

Julie: Why?

Therapist: Because I am going to miss you a lot.

Julie: (softly) And what's the other reason?

Therapist: Because I've really had fun playing with you and I think you do really good stories that are important.

Julie: My stories *are* important.

Therapist: Do you want me to tell you what I think of your story today? . . . Come here. I want to tell you about it.

Julie. No. I can hear it from here. (standing in doorway)

Therapist: Oh, I wish you could be here with me.

Julie: How about I sit right here? (sits across the room)

Therapist: Let me show you what I think. . . . You know, you know who I think is you in this story today?

Julie: Who? (moves closer to sandtray)

Therapist: I think this is you. (holds up the strongest of the sisters)

Julie: Yep. (moves closer, standing next to therapist and sandtray)

Therapist: Am I right? (Julie nods) . . . And you know what I think of that? . . . I think that this is a very strong girl. She was so strong in the story that she took care of everything, didn't she?

Julie: (sounding better) Yes, she did.

Therapist: Everything that happened that was gonna be bad, she took care of it. Even Batman couldn't take care of it.

Julie: (laughing) No way. Batman couldn't take care of it at all.

Therapist: She . . . and she reminds me so much of you.
Julie: And I wish I had a fox.
Therapist: Yeah, I know you do.

Julie leaves the room again. When her father persuades her again to return, she cries that now her arms are too tired, and that is what she is upset about, and that is why she cannot clean up.

Therapist: Your arms are hurting. I know. We've done a lot of work today, haven't we?
Julie: Yeah. And that's why I don't want to clean up.
Therapist: Yeah. You've done a lot of work. And you know what, Julie? I get to see you in two days.
Julie: I don't care!
Therapist: You don't care?
Julie: (tearfully) I just . . . I . . . I . . . All I wanna do . . . is not clean up and my arms are still tired.

Finally, in our last session, Julie was able to verbalize what she was feeling about terminating. She had begun crying because she wanted to do one more thing, but we were out of time and we needed to clean up.

Julie: I just want to try out something.
Therapist: Well, it's not going to work and right now it's time to clean up.
Julie: I don't care.
Therapist: I know. The endings are hard for you lately, aren't they? . . .
Julie: That's 'cause I don't want to make an ending.

Therapist: I know. I know the endings are hard and you
     don't want it to end right now, right?
Julie: I don't want it to end at all.

Julie's incredible insight contributed to her healing. The
following exchange was during our second-to-last session,
another in which Julie created a story about sisters who
saved baby animals from a wicked witch.

Therapist: Julie, your stories are so good and so
     important.
Julie: I know. They're supposed to teach about my
     mom. . . . And they do.

At this point one has to ask, who is teaching whom?

14

Putting the Puzzle Together: Concluding Remarks

Working with children is like putting together a puzzle. We have a notion of what the picture is supposed to look like, and we begin by setting up the boundary, finding those straight edges that are easy to see and will keep the picture contained. As we work, we realize that we don't have all the pieces we need. We search for clues that will help us to understand the puzzle, knowing that the pieces that worked for the last puzzle probably aren't going to fit here. This book has delineated some of the complexities of work with children and opens the door for further dialogue about how we can best meet treatment needs. A combination of looking at issues from an object relations, cognitive behavioral, and family systems perspective has been suggested. Each case is unique, and despite an attempt to categorize some of the treatment issues here, it is understood that each case ultimately truly is its own puzzle with its own pieces.

When children come into therapy, it is important to realize that they are resilient and that their defense mechanisms may have worked well for them. Therapists need to preserve these defenses until the child is ready to relinquish them. Using art and play allows the child an opportunity to express the conflict in safe and contained ways, experiment with different outcomes, and become empowered, thus decreasing reliance on old defenses. It is not in the child's best interest, and will often be counterproductive, to push him to talk before he is ready.

I recommend that child therapists receive training in art and play therapy in order to meet the treatment needs of children from early childhood through latency. At adolescence, the child is more capable of processing on a verbal level, although many adolescents are at their peak of creativity and can make tremendous use of poetry, art, drama, and other expressive modalities. Always, the therapist needs to understand how cognitive and psychological development overlap and interrelate.

Because of children's investment in *not* talking, the highly defended nature of the issues, and the often excellent coping skills that have helped them to survive, alternative means of expression that allow for communication of intense feelings without words are crucial. The opportunity for reenactment within the therapy setting is important because it provides an alternative for the child who is acting out inappropriately. A cognitive behavioral approach is used to help the child when he is acting out inappropriately at home or at school.

This book suggests that therapists define treatment issues to coincide with developmental stages. It centers around a hope that the treatment does not reflect our need to process issues at a level the child is not yet capable of. The therapist supports the child's attachment, but also his individuation. There is an implicit hope of promoting the idea of health and a natural progression of treatment, rather than pathologizing the child. At each stage the child progresses through a series of treatment issues that coincide with the developmental issues of that stage. The child will progress only so far at each stage, and then, if there is a strong support system available for him, therapy may be terminated until he is ready to process at a new level. The *practicing period* that the child engages in while not in therapy is a time to consolidate gains made in therapy, and engage in age-appropriate experiences. A child will usually indicate, through behavior or signs of anxiety, that therapy should be resumed.

When a therapist makes a commitment to work with children, the commitment includes a lot more than just being present with the child client. The therapist must communicate with many people in the child's life in order to put together the puzzle, possibly including families, the protective services social worker, foster families, teachers, and residential treatment center staff. The therapist may have to balance between being the child's advocate and working with the systems that affect the child. In many cases the work will be futile without family involvement. In other cases, because there is no available family, attachment issues are paramount.

There are no set answers and there is no technique that will be universally effective. A technique that was created by one child through the course of therapy is likely to be useless for another. The therapist must learn to think creatively and be responsive to the child. Children will gravitate toward forms of expression that will help them to communicate feelings safely. The therapist must watch and follow where the child is leading.

The strength these children demonstrate is amazing and it can touch the therapist in many ways. The children's stories and artwork presented here humble us with their teachings about symbolism. When we learn to trust the process, we help children find their paths.

Epilogue:
The Therapist's Container

I draw pictures about my clients for many reasons. Sometimes I just need to release the images. I have found myself purging myself of my clients' stories because I cannot contain them anymore. At those times I do not need feedback; I just need to let go of images that frighten me or make me angry. Figure E–1 is such a picture. It is about a highly sexualized, emotionally hurt little 5-year-old girl and a foster mother who was ready to adopt her. However, before adoption could take place, a grandmother, who had been absent from the child's life almost since birth, emerged and wanted to have her. I was angry at everyone: the protective services system, the grandmother, the mother, the foster family. I wanted to scream in frustration that two years of therapy and really good foster parenting could be so quickly destroyed. I used this picture to vent my frustration and anger. I did not need to dwell on this piece of art, I just needed to create

Figure E–1. Therapist's drawing of countertransference feelings

it. More often, I need to look at the artwork to understand what my feelings are.

It is useful, in this sense, to think of the art as a container (Allen 1988). Having that witness, which Allen (1995) describes as necessary to images, helps the therapist to see feelings without the censorship that is so easy when using only words. Looking to the images for meaning helps the therapist to understand his or her clients better, through understanding countertransference and projective identifications.

Work with children who have experienced early trauma is difficult and challenges the therapist on many levels. Countertransference reactions that are unique to this kind of work are experienced, and include denial, detachment, enmeshment, overcommitment, rescuer activities, withdrawal, and codependent relations (Wilson and Lindy 1994, Wilson et al. 1994).

Supervision, even for seasoned therapists, is vitally important. Supervision provides the distance that the therapist needs to look at cases objectively. Because these stories are emotionally laden, the therapist must also find some way of containing the client's pain so that it does not overwhelm the therapist.

MAKING ART ABOUT THE THERAPEUTIC RELATIONSHIP

Making art about the therapeutic relationship can help the therapist see those unconscious or denied aspects of the countertransference. When the therapist draws or sculpts the therapist–client relationship, it releases feelings that may be difficult to grasp. Once these feelings are made into images, it allows the therapist enough physical and emotional distance to approach the countertransference more objectively. These images can then be processed to help the therapist organize his or her thoughts about a client. "Surprises" often emerge through the image that provide deeper insight into the therapist–client relationship. We can learn from what emerges in the art.

> I chose to focus on the S. family in a workshop dealing with countertransference issues, led by Franklin (1995). The workshop was designed to help therapists create the observing ego through art, and to use this psychological distance as a means of developing inner awareness. The directive in the experiential aspect of the workshop was to draw a client, then draw how we feel about the client, and then draw

a holding environment, or the space that these two people share. Finally, we were to place the drawings in the environment we created, thinking about placement, and how the images overlapped or required distance.

I drew about a difficult case. Sam, an explosive 10-year-old boy, was referred and brought to therapy by his mother. During our first session, he spent the entire hour in my waiting room. He refused to enter my office and did everything possible to get his mother to leave as well. He was very adept at his games, and alternated between being angry, tearful, and manipulative. When angry, he hit and kicked his mother and shouted at her, calling her stupid. He frustrated me. I like to think I am good with children, but I could not get him to come into my office.

I drew my client exploding off the page, extremely angry and emotional. I drew my feelings about the client to reflect my frustration with him, my anger and rage at his behavior. Visually, the pictures I drew of him and of myself could have been interchangeable. The projective identification was my rage and frustration toward him, which echoed his rage and frustration toward his mother. He was making me feel like he must feel all the time.

When a therapist is stuck with a client, it is useful to use countertransference feelings to understand what is happening in the therapy. Duncan (1981) suggests that the therapist will experience a thought, sensation, or feeling in response to the client's material that is a reflection of the projective and introjective processes. When the therapist experiences the same feeling state as that of the client, countertransference feelings that can be useful to the therapy are experienced by the therapist. It is important that the therapist not be damaged, hurt, or changed by the projection, but rather be able to contain it for the client, so that it can become neutralized. Art provides a way to understand, and helps to put the feelings in a place outside of the self where they can be acknowledged.

I was ambivalent about this drawing of the client. It tossed around in the trunk of my car for three or four days and then I moved it to my office, still rolled up. My plan was to take it to supervision and discuss it further. However, when I went to unroll it and flatten it out, I could not remember the meanings I had assigned to what I had drawn, or even what the directives were for the picture. I also was annoyed because the materials I had chosen were so messy, the charcoal was smearing, and it was too much work to get the rolled up picture flattened out. It (he!) was just too messy to deal with! I tossed the picture in the trash.

The fact that I threw the picture away should have been my sign that it was an important piece for me to process. But avoidance is a wonderful defense and I had many other cases to discuss in supervision.

As the therapy progressed I found myself feeling confused as to who my client actually was. Sam's anger about coming changed. He continued to resist coming and threw tantrums prior to our sessions, but once at my office, he allowed himself to become engaged in art making. I used part of his sessions to work with his mother on behavior management techniques. Then, when I tried to ally myself with Sam, I realized that he could not fully trust me.

As I became more confused, I decided to face the case more directly. I drew the child and I drew our relationship again (see Figure E–2). Sam was so angry and so controlling. My picture reflects the child's dilemma. I did the picture without conscious thought and then reflected upon what the picture might mean. In this picture, the child, in the upper left, explodes. The figure of the therapist (right) reaches out to help the child, and reaches out to help the mother. But both attempts are blocked because of the mother's power. Her pivotal position allows her to control the relationships. So Sam, who also attempts to control through his behavior, continues to master ways of manipulation and anger to get his needs met. Ultimately, I was unable to penetrate the dynamics of this system. The mother decided she wanted individual sessions for herself instead of Sam, so we could

E–2. Therapist's drawing of countertransference feelings

talk about his behavior. She had a litany of complaints ready for me. I allowed the mother to be in control of the therapy, and she announced the following session that it would be our last meeting.

I became painfully aware that by not actively responding to my feelings in time, I missed an important communication from the clients, and the therapy could not continue. Obviously my clients could not speak of their dilemma, for they had developed a system that worked for their family. As long as I did not institute change, everyone knew what was expected and, as frustrating and maddening as the mother claimed her son's behavior was, she perpetuated the problem. Each family member had a role to play within that system.

In this case, Sam could never articulate his frustration with a mother who could not nurture him. Sam could only explode his frustrations through controlling behavior that was designed to control his mother. When I responded to this case through my own art I became aware of the projective identification, and only then did I understand Sam's dilemma. Unfortunately, in this case it was too late.

The clues that I was missing were held in the countertransference. I, too, felt out of control and frustrated. I allowed the mother to control me through her insistence upon individual sessions to talk about the "problem child." Unbeknownst to me, I was colluding with her. After I drew the picture, which was quickly done, without conscious thought, I was able to look at it more objectively, and understand the dynamics that had been lost on me earlier. This method of objectifying the countertransference provides a way for the therapist to process with him- or herself.

My drawing in this example taught me the importance of setting firmer boundaries with a client such as this. How is it that the mother had so much control in our therapeutic relationship? Looking back, I realized the peculiarities of this case. I was attempting to do family therapy without demanding that the whole family be present. I was doing art therapy, but the mother never participated in doing art. Because the mother scheduled herself for parenting consultation so often, I found myself only seeing the child once a month. It is no wonder that I could not truly meet the child. It is also no wonder that I, too, did not want to nurture the child.

THERAPIST'S ART MAKING TO ENHANCE EMPATHY

I drew what the experience must have been like for my clients. A mother and her twin boys were held hostage by an intruder. The ordeal ended when the intruder forced them into the mother's car at gunpoint, and made her drive to a parking lot. As the intruder held the gun to the mother's head, a police marksman shot and killed him, leaving the mother unscathed.

Somehow, I was having a difficult time being empathic with the story, because the mother presented the case so articulately and unemotionally, with little apparent trauma, and minimized the impact that it had on her. It was not until I drew what the ordeal must have felt like that I was able to understand the mother's fear and panic, which she and I were successfully denying.

One risk in working with trauma over many years is the desensitization of the therapist. If the client denies, the therapist can also deny. The words written in the social history section of the client's file begin to have no meaning. One can describe a case in clinical terms and not feel the power of the words any longer. But there is a risk involved in this. The risk is that the therapist, in order to protect him- or herself from these repeated stories, cannot feel empathy. Sometimes it takes effort to be empathic.

The therapist's lack of empathy can become a way of protecting him or her from vicarious trauma. We do exactly what our clients do; we numb ourselves from the pain. One cannot hear these stories, read these case histories, and experience the trauma through the art and play without being affected. Particularly when it involves children, the horrendous nature of the acts is difficult to contain. Art can help us feel empathy.

THE THERAPIST'S ART AS A CONTAINER FOR THE COUNTERTRANSFERENCE

The artwork that is produced in therapy serves as a transitional object and holds the client (Robbins and Cooper 1993). This unique aspect of art therapy occurs despite the transference and countertransference interactions that go on between the therapist and client. Art can also serve as a transitional object for the therapist, when using art therapeutically in supervision. The therapist's art holds the image of the therapist–client relationship, which the therapist can then process with a supervisor sensitive to creative process and image-making.

I have a client who eludes me in her sophisticated and refined use of dissociation. She has me convinced at times, despite evidence from the Federal Bureau of Investigation of her involvement in child pornography and her known association with a cult, that she was never abused. Hearing the details of her case traumatizes me, but she presents herself extraordinarily well, like a normal teenager. I made a sculpture of my feelings about what it must be like to live in her body. These are my projections. The sculpture is about her pain and my feelings about her pain. I identify with the part of her that denies the pain. The sculpture is about the three sides to Sharon: the side she presents, represented by a bright eye in a light blue and yellow sky; the side that got abused and threatened, which is a bound and gagged face amid red and black slashes; and the side that dissociated, which is a midnight blue, floating eye that shows no feeling. Fourteen nails on the perimeter of the sculpture represent the 14 years of her life. The sculpture is precariously held together with materials that do not seem to work well. Intellectually, I know how to use sculptural materials for more permanency, but I somehow failed to do so in this piece. It is fragile and falls apart as I carry it. Now it is held together by thin silver threads, as is my client.

I experience vicarious trauma with this client. I draw images that she has never shown me, yet I know are there. I worry about instilling false memories with her, and am careful not to make any suggestions to her. I use only words that she has given me, and do not ask direct questions. Were it not for so much concrete evidence, which we often do not have in child abuse cases, I would not believe her situation.

Kluft (1994) talks about the unique types of countertransference issues in work with dissociative clients. These include feelings of frustration and exasperation in respone to the client's world of dissociation, the client's preoccupation with pain evasion, and the client's preoccupation with controlling the therapist. These issues will come up periodically in the therapy, and the therapist who can be aware of projective identifications will best be able to meet these issues. This kind of frustration and exasperation can take the form of the therapist's repression or enmeshment, neither of which is healthy for the therapy (Wilson and Lindy 1994). By staying with the image, the therapist can circumvent repression of the feelings evoked.

When drawing about clients, it helps the therapist to understand what his or her feelings are, especially in cases where one feels overwhelmed and does not want to risk feeling too much. Robbins (1987) suggests that both the therapist and the client are in treatment within the art-therapy relationship. Robbins hopes that the therapist will be more in charge of the process than the clients, "but the therapist should not fool himself with false notions of professionalism or objectivity" (p. 150). Consequently, the sometimes fine lines between supervision and therapy, and client–therapist issues can also be contained through the use of the therapist's artwork in supervision. The supervisor witnesses and reacts to the artwork. The reaction to the image by someone not involved in the case adds an uncontaminated and objective viewpoint. The supervisor's emotional reaction to the image can reveal aspects of the countertransference that are contained in the image.

Working with abused children makes one appreciate their incredible survival instincts. I am astounded at the children's ability to contain their own pain. Before I did my sculpture of Sharon, I felt vicarious trauma; I was taking in her pain of loss and rejection, which is even worse than the physical pain of being burned, beaten, or sexually abused. This kind of work is very difficult.

USE OF ART TO HOLD THE AMBIGUITY OF NOT KNOWING

Particularly with abused children, the therapist may not have all of the information necessary to make an accurate assessment, and the child's idiosyncratic use of symbols in art and play may be difficult to decipher at first. The therapist must be able to tolerate and hold the ambiguity of not knowing. The therapist must go where the child is leading. Bollas (1987), although he is not an art therapist, speaks to the power of the image and nonverbal processes. Bollas recognizes the difficulties clients have in expressing preverbal thoughts and longings in words when they may have no cognitive memory of the longings. He devised the term *the unthought known*, which refers to reliving early memories of being and relating through language of that which is known, but not yet thought. He sees the unthought known as being integrally connected to the aesthetic moment, such as through a painting, a poem, or music. This aesthetic experience is an existential recollection of the time when communicating took place through this illusion of deep rapport of subject and object. The full articulation of preverbal transference evolves in the therapist's countertransference.

When the client cannot express the conflict in words, the transference–countertransference interaction can be an expression of the unthought known. Bollas feels that the infant element in the client speaks to the therapist through object usage that is revealed through the therapist's countertransference, and that the therapist should, in fact, allow the client to affect him or her. In fact, he advocates that the therapist become disturbed by the client. The therapist who can identify his or her own feelings in relationship to the client can use this countertransferential material to benefit the therapy. Just as clients relive early memories and preverbal feelings of the unthought known in their art, the therapist, through creating art, can better understand the unthought known of the countertransference.

> I drew Julie (see Figure E–3), my 4-year-old client whose mother shot her. I find myself so emotionally tied up when I think of her at times. After drawing, I meditate on my picture for several minutes, and try to learn from it. Then I write:

E–3. Therapist's drawing of countertransference feelings

She is so vulnerable.
She doesn't have a chance.
My "rescue" fantasies are activated and then I feel
Powerless
Helpless
Useless.
Her life has been black and red.
I want to break through and make it better,
And I am faced with my own limitations.
What can I learn here?
I can touch her, but I cannot take her out of this space.
I've drawn myself as a tree—
Firmly rooted, but unable to move,
Extending a limb, but unable to hold onto her.
Only able to touch.
Hopefully, it will help.
I can do what I do best—
Touch, nurture, be with her.
I cannot do more—
Change
Move
Rescue.

The art helps me to understand my rescue fantasies. It helps me articulate the unthought known, that place beyond words, where I find myself emotionally tied up. Releasing these feelings into the art helps me to accept my own limitations. The art becomes a container for me.

Appendix A:
Children's Books

There may be a time in therapy when the child cannot tolerate talking directly about what troubles him or her, but is receptive to reading books about similar circumstances or feelings. A few books I have found helpful are included here.

Adams, C., and Fay, J. (1984). *Nobody Told Me It Was Rape*. Santa Cruz, CA: Network Publications.

Boegehold, B. (1985). *You Can Say "No."* Racine, WI: Western Publishing.

Cain, B. S. (1990). *Double-dip Feelings*. New York: Magination Press.

Carlson, N. (1988). *I Like Me*. New York: Viking.

Coalition for Child Advocacy. (1985). *Touching*. Lynnwood, WA: Whatcom Opportunity Council and Bergsma Collectibles.

Crary, E. (1992). *I'm Frustrated*. Seattle, WA: Parenting Press.

Dayee, F. S. (1982). *Private Zone*. New York: Warner.

Fay, J. J., and Flerchinger, B. J. (1982). *Top Secret*. Kent, WA: King County Rape Relief.

Freeman, L. (1982). *It's My Body*. Seattle, WA: Parenting Press.

Gil, E. (1986). *I Told My Secret*. Rockville, MD: Launch Press.

Girard, L. W. (1984). *My Body Is Private*. Morton Grove, IL: Albert Whitman.

—— (1985). *Who Is a Stranger and What Should I Do?* Morton Grove, IL: Albert Whitman.

Gordon, S., and Gordon, J. (1984). *A Better Safe Than Sorry Book*. Buffalo, NY: Prometheus Books.

Heidemann, S. (1997). *A Safe Place for Michael and Sara*. Minneapolis, MN: University of Minnesota Press.

—— (1997). *Together Again*. Minneapolis, MN: University of Minnesota Press.

—— (1997). *Two Places Called Home*. Minneapolis, MN: University of Minnesota Press.

Hoke, S. (1995). *My Body Is Mine, My Feelings Are Mine*. King of Prussia, PA: The Center for Applied Psychology.

Illinois Coalition Against Sexual Assault. (1990). *Acquaintance Rape*. Springfield, IL: Illinois Coalition Against Sexual Assault.

Johnson, K. (1986). *The Trouble with Secrets*. Seattle, WA: Parenting Press.

Katz, I. (1994). *Sarah*. Northridge, CA: Real Life Storybooks.

Laskin, P. L., and Moskowitz, A. A. (1991). *Wish Upon a Star*. New York: Magination Press.

Levy, B. (1984). *Skills for Violence-Free Relationships*. Santa Monica, CA: Southern California Coalition on Battered Women.

Mast, C. K. (1986). *Sex Respect*. Golf, IL: Project Respect.

Porett, J. (1993). *When I Was Little Like You*. Washington, DC: Child Welfare League of America.

Sanford, D. (1986). *I Can't Talk About It*. Hong Kong: Multnomah Press.

—— (1993). *Something Must Be Wrong with Me*. Hong Kong: Gold'n'Honey Books.

Stanek, M. (1983). *Don't Hurt Me, Mama.* Niles, IL: Albert Whitman.

Sweet, P. E. (1981). *Something Happened To Me.* Racine, WI: Mother Courage Press.

Terkel, S. N., and Rench, J. E. (1984). *Feeling Safe, Feeling Strong.* Minneapolis, MN: Lerner Publications.

Appendix B:
Resources for Therapists

Childswork Childsplay, P.O. Box 1604, Secaucus, NJ 07096-1604. 1-800-962-1141. Fax 1-201-583-3644. Books, games, doll houses and families, puppets, anatomically correct dolls, therapy materials.

Kidsrights, 10100 Park Cedar Drive, Suite 100, Charlotte, NC 28210. 1-888-970-5437, or 704-541-0100. Fax 704-541-0113. Books, games, dollhouses and families, puppets, anatomically correct dolls, therapy materials.

Nasco, 901 Janesville Ave., Fort Atkinson, WI 53538-0901. 1-920-563-2446. Fax 920-563-8296. Art supplies of every kind.

Playrooms, P.O. Box 2660, Petaluma, CA 94953. 1-800-667-2470. Fax 1-707-763-8353. Sandtrays and sandtray miniatures.

Sportime, One Sportime Way, Atlanta, GA 30340-1402. 1-800-850-8602. Fax 1-770-263-0897. Co-Oper Bands™, Physioballs, and other movement therapy props.

Sterns Books, 2004 West Roscoe Street, Chicago, IL 60618. 773-883-5100. Fax 773-477-6096. Books on art and other expressive therapies; books for children, anatomical dolls, puppets, and therapeutic games.

Appendix C:
Additional Readings

Agell, G., Levick, M., Rhyne, J., et al. (1981). Transference and countertransference in art therapy. *American Journal of Art Therapy,* 2(17):3–24.

Besharov, D. (1994). Responding to child sexual abuse: the need for a balanced approach. In *The Future of Children: Sexual Abuse of Children*, ed., R. Behrman, pp. 135–155. Los Altos, CA: Center for the Future of Children, the David and Lucille Packard Foundation.

Blain, G. H., Bergner, R. M., Lewis, M. L., and Goldstein, M. A. (1981). The use of objectively scorable house-tree-person indicators to establish child abuse. *Journal of Clinical Psychology* 37 (3):667–673.

Chandler, M., and Greenspan, S. (1972). Ersatz egocentrism: a reply to H. Borke. *Developmental Psychology* 7(2):104–106.

Cohen, B. M., Hammer, J. S. and Singer, S. (1988). The Diagnostic Drawing Series: a systematic approach to art therapy evaluation and research. *Arts in Psychotherapy* 15(1):11–21.

Cohen, F. W., and Phelps, R. E. (1985). Incest markers in children's artwork. *Arts in Psychotherapy* 12:265–283.

Cohn, A. H., and Daro, D. (1987). Is treatment too late?: What ten years of evaluative research tell us. *Child Abuse and Neglect* 11(3):433–442.

Culbertson, F. M., and Revel, A. C. (1987). Graphic characteristics on the Draw-a-Person test for identification of physical abuse. *Art Therapy* 4(2):78–83.

Deblinger, E., McLeer, S. V., and Henry, D. (1990). Cognitive behavioral treatment for sexually abused children suffering post-traumatic stress: preliminary findings. *Journal of the American Academy of Child and Adolescent Psychiatry* 29(5):747–752.

Finkelhor, D. (1994). Current information on the scope and nature of child sexual abuse. In *The Future of Children: Sexual Abuse of Children* ed. R. Behrman, pp. 31–53. Los Altos, CA: Center for the Future of Children, the David and Lucille Packard Foundation.

Finkelhor, D., and Baron, L. (1986). High-risk children. In *A Sourcebook on Child Sexual Abuse*, ed. D. Finkelhor, pp. 60–88. Beverly Hills, CA: Sage.

Gantt, E. (1994). *How do pictures mean?* Keynote address at the Spring Art Therapy Conference at Southern Illinois University at Edwardsville, IL, April.

Greenspan, S. I., and Greenspan, N. T. (1985). *First Feelings: Milestones in the Emotional Development of Your Baby and Child.* New York: Viking Penguin.

Greenspan, S. I., and Lourie, R. S. (1981). Developmental structuralist approach to the classification of adaptive and pathologic personality organizations: infancy and early childhood. *American Journal of Psychiatry* 138(6):725–735.

Howard, A. C. (1986). Developmental play ages of physically abused and nonabused children. *American Journal of Occupational Therapy*, 40 (10): 691–695.

Johnson, T. C. (1989). Female child perpetators: childen who molest other children. *Child Abuse and Neglect* 13:571–585.

———— (1991). Children who molest children: identification and
treatment approaches for children who molest other children.
The American Professional Society on the Abuse of Children (Fall),
pp. 9–11.

———— (1991). Understanding the sexual behaviors of young children. *SIECUS Report* (August/September), pp. 8–15.

Karen, R. (1977). *Becoming Attached.* New York: Warner.

Kaufman, B., and Wohl, A. (1992). *Casualties of Childhood: A Developmental Perspective on Sexual Abuse Using Projective Drawings.* New York: Brunner/Mazel.

Koppitz, E. M. (1968). *Psychological Evaluation of Children's Human
Figure Drawings.* New York: Grune & Stratton.

Levick, M. F., Safran, D., and Levine, A. (1990). Art therapists as
expert witnesses: a judge delivers a precedent-setting decision.
Arts in Psychotherapy 17:49–53.

Levitt, E., & Pinnell, C. M. (1995). Some additional light on the
childhood sexual abuse-psychopathology axis. *International
Journal of Clinical and Experimental Hypnosis* 43(2):145–162.

Lewit, E. (1994). Reported child abuse and neglect. In *The Future
of Children: Sexual Abuse of Children,* ed. R. Behrman, pp. 233–
242. Los Altos, CA: Center for the Future of Children, the David
and Lucille Packard Foundation.

Lyons, S. J. (1993). Art psychotherapy evaluations of children in
custody disputes. *Arts in Psychotherapy* 20:153–159.

Mahler, M. (1979). *The Selected Papers of Margaret S. Mahler: Infantile
Psychosis and Early Contributions.* New York: Jason Aronson.

———— (1979). *The Selected Papers of Margaret S. Mahler: Separation-Individuation.* New York: Jason Aronson.

Mahler, M., Pine, F., and Bergman, A. (1975). *The Psychological Birth
of the Human Infant: Symbiosis and Individuation.* New York:
Basic Books.

Manning, T. M. (1987). Aggression depicted in abused children's drawings. *Arts in Psychotherapy* 14:15–24.

Myers, J. E. (1996). Expert testimony. In *American Professional Society on the Abuse of Children Handbook on Child Maltreatment*, ed. J. Briere, L. Berliner, J. Bulkley, et al., pp. 319–340. Thousand Oaks, CA: Sage.

Peterson, L. W., Hardin, M., and Nitsch, M. J. (1995). The use of children's drawings in the evaluation and treatment of child sexual, emotional, and physical abuse. *Archives of Family Medicine* 4:445–452.

Pine, F. (1985). *Developmental Theory and Clinical Process*. New Haven: Yale University Press.

Riley, S. (1985). Draw me a paradox? . . . family art psychotherapy utilizing a systematic approach to change. *Art Therapy* 2:116–123.

Scharff, D. E., and Scharff, J. S. (1991). *Object Relations Family Therapy*. Northvale, NJ: Jason Aronson.

Scharff, J. S. (1992). *Projective and Introjective Identification and the Use of the Therapist's Self*. Northvale, NJ: Jason Aronson.

Sgroi, S. (1982). *Handbook of Clinical Intervention in Child Sexual Abuse*. Lexington, MA: Lexington Books.

Sidun, N. M., and Rosenthal, R. H. (1987). Graphic indicators of sexual abuse in Draw-a-Person tests of psychiatrically hospitalized adolescents. *Arts in Psychotherapy* 14:25–33.

U. S. Department of Health and Human Services. (1992). *National child abuse and neglect data system: 1990 summary data component*. Working paper No. 1. National Center on Child Abuse and Neglect.

Yates, A., Beutler, L. E., and Crago, M. (1985). Drawings by child victims of incest. *Child Abuse and Neglect* 9(2):183–190.

Zaidi, L. Y., and Gutierrez-Kovner, V. (1995). Group treatment of sexually abused latency-age girls. *Journal of Interpersonal Violence* 10(2):215–227.

References

Ackerman, F., Colapinto, J. A., Scharf, C. N., et al. (1991). The involuntary client: avoiding "pretend therapy." *Family Systems Medicine* 9 (3):261–266.

Allen, P. B. (1988). A consideration of transference in art therapy. *American Journal of Art Therapy* 26:113–118.

——— (1995). *Art Is a Way of Knowing.* Boston: Shambhala.

American Psychiatric Association. (1994). *Diagnostic and Statistical Manual of Mental Disorders* (4th ed.). Washington, DC: Author.

Beutler, L., Williams, R., and Zetzer, H. (1994). Efficacy of treatment for victims of child sexual abuse. In *The Future of Children: Sexual Abuse of Children* ed. R. Behrman, pp. 156–175. Los Altos, CA: Center for the Future of Children, the David and Lucille Packard Foundation.

Blos, P. (1962). *On Adolescence: A Psychoanalytic Interpretation.* New York: Free Press.

Bollas, C. (1987). *The Shadow of the Object: Psychoanalysis of the Unthought Known.* New York: Columbia University Press.

Borke, H. (1971). Interpersonal perception of young children: Egocentrism or empathy? *Developmental Psychology* 5(2):263–269.

———— (1972). Chandler and Greenspan's "Ersatz Egocentrism": a rejoinder. *Developmental Psychology* 7(2):107–109.

Bowlby, J. (1969). *Attachment* (second ed.). New York: Basic Books.

———— (1973). *Separation: Anxiety and Anger.* New York: Basic Books.

Braun, B., and Sachs, R. (1985). The development of multiple personality disorder. In *Childhood Antecedents of Multiple Personality*, ed. R. Kluft, pp. 38–64. Washington DC: American Psychiatric Press.

Briere, J., and Elliott, D. (1994). Immediate and long-term impacts of child sexual abuse. In *The Future of Children: Sexual Abuse of Children*, ed. R. Behrman, pp. 54–69. Los Altos, CA: Center for the Future of Children, the David and Lucille Packard Foundation.

Buck, J. (1985). *The House-Tree-Person Technique: Revised Manual.* Los Angeles: Western Psychological Services.

Burns, R. (1987). *Kinetic-House-Tree-Person Drawings (K-H-T-P): An Interpretive Manual.* New York: Brunner/Mazel.

Cairns, R. B. (1966a). Attachment behavior of mammals. *Psychological Review* 73:409–426.

———— (1966b). Development, maintenance, and extinction of social attachment behavior in sheep. *Journal of Comparative Physiological Psychology* 62:298–306.

Carlson, N. (1988). *I Like Me.* New York: Viking.

Dawson, B., Vaughan, A. R., and Wagner, W. G. (1992). Normal responses to sexually anatomically detailed dolls. *Journal of Family Violence* 7(2):135–152.

Duncan, D. (1981). A thought on the nature of psychoanalytic theory. *International Journal of Psycho-Analysis* 62:339–349.

Fairbairn, W. R. D. (1941). *An Object-Relations Theory of the Personality.* New York: Basic Books.

Famularo, R., Kinscherff, R., and Fenton, T. (1990). Symptom differences in acute and chronic presentation of childhood post-traumatic stress disorder. *Child Abuse and Neglect* 14:439–444.

Franklin, M. (1995). *Becoming a student of oneself: activating the internal witness as a guide in supervision.* Keynote address at the Spring Art Therapy Conference at Southern Illinois University at Edwardsville, IL, April.

Freud, A. (1981). A psychoanalyst's view of sexual abuse by parents. In *Sexually Abused Children and Their Families*, ed. P. B. Mrazek and C. H. Kempe, pp. 33–34. New York: Pergamon.

Friedrich, W. N. (1990). *Psychotherapy of Sexually Abused Children and Their Families.* New York: Norton.

—— (1993a). Sexual behavior in sexually abused children. *Violence Update* 3(5):7–12.

—— (1993b). Sexual victimization and sexual behavior in children: a review of the literature. *Child Abuse and Neglect*, 17:59–66.

Friedrich, W. N., Grambsch, P., Broughton, D., et al. (1991). Normative sexual behavior in children. *Pediatrics* 88:456–464.

Friedrich, W. N., Grambsch, P., Damon, L., et al. (1992). Child sexual behavior inventory: normative and clinical comparisons. *Psychological Assessment* 4:303–311.

Furniss, T. (1984). Organizing a therapeutic approach to inter-familial child sexual abuse. *Journal of Adolescence* 7(4):309–317.

Gantt, L., and Tabone, C. (1998). *The Formal Elements Art Therapy Scale.* Morgantown, WV: Gargoyle.

Gil, E., and Johnson, T. C. (1993). *Sexualized Children: Assessment and Treatment of Sexualized Children and Children Who Molest.* New York: Launch.

Gomes-Schwartz, B., Horowitz, J. M., and Sauzier, M. (1985). Severity of emotional distress among sexually abused preschool,

school-age, and adolescent children. *Hospital and Community Psychiatry* 36(5):503–508.

Green, A. H. (1985). Children traumatized by physical abuse. In *Post-Traumatic Stress Disorder in Children*, ed. S. Eth and R. S. Pynoos, pp. 135–154. Washington, DC: American Psychiatric Press.

Greenspan, S. I. (1979). *Intelligence and Adaptation: An Integration of Psychoanalytic and Piagetian Developmental Psychology.* New York: International Universities Press.

Hammer, E. F. (1958). *The Clinical Application of Projective Drawings.* Springfield, IL: Charles C Thomas.

Harvey, S. (1990). Dynamic play therapy: an integrative expressive arts approach to the family therapy of young children. *The Arts in Psychotherapy* 17:239–246.

——— (1991). Creating a family: an integrated expressive approach to adoption. *The Arts in Psychotherapy* 18:213–222.

Jernberg, A. (1979). *Theraplay: A New Treatment Using Structured Play for Problem Children and Their Families.* San Francisco: Jossey-Bass.

Katz, I. (1994). *Sarah.* Northridge, CA: Real Life Storybooks.

Kellogg, R. (1970). *Analyzing Children's Art.* Palo Alto, CA: Mayfield.

Kiser, L. J., Heston, J., Millsap, P. A., and Pruitt, D. B. (1991). Physical and sexual abuse in childhood: relationship with post-traumatic stress disorder. *Journal of the American Academy of Child and Adolescent Psychiatry* 30(5):776–783.

Klorer, G. (1995). Use of anatomical dolls in play and art therapy with sexually abused children. *The Arts in Psychotherapy* 22(5):467–473.

Kluft, R. (1994). Countertransference in the treatment of multiple personality disorder. In *Countertransference in the Treatment of PTSD*, ed. J. Wilson and J. Lindy, pp. 122–150. New York: Guilford.

Kramer, E. (1971). *Art as Therapy with Children.* New York: Schocken.

Kwiatkowska, H. (1978). *Family Therapy and Evaluation through Art.* Springfield, IL: Charles C Thomas.

Landgarten, H. (1987). *Family Art Psychotherapy.* New York: Brunner/Mazel.

Levick, M. (1983). *They Could Not Talk and So They Drew: Children's Styles of Coping and Thinking.* Springfield, IL: Charles C Thomas.

——— (1989). *The Levick emotional and cognitive art therapy assessment.* (Available from Myra Levick, 21710 Palm Circle, Boca Raton, FL 33433).

Liang, B., Bogat, A., and McGrath, M. (1993). Differential understanding of sexual abuse prevention concepts among preschoolers. *Child Abuse and Neglect* 17(5):641–650.

Linesch, D. (1993). *Art Therapy with Families in Crisis.* New York: Brunner/Mazel.

Lowenfeld, V., and Brittain, W. (1987). *Creative and Mental Growth.* New York: Macmillan.

MacKinnon, L., and James, K. (1992a). Raising the stakes in child-at-risk cases: eliciting and maintaining parents' motivation. *Australian and New Zealand Journal of Family Therapy* 13(2):59–71.

——— (1992b). Working with "the Welfare" in child-at-risk cases. *Australian and New Zealand Journal of Family Therapy* 13(1):1–15.

Malchiodi, C. (1990). *Breaking the Silence: Art Therapy with Children from Violent Homes.* New York: Brunner/Mazel.

May, R. (1975). *The Courage to Create.* New York: Norton.

Nader, K., and Pynoos, R. S. (1991). Play and drawing techniques as tools for interviewing traumatized children. In *Play Diagnosis and Assessment,* ed. C. E. Schaefer, K. Gitlin, and A. Sandgrund, pp. 375–389. New York: Wiley.

Pardeck, J. T. (1988). Family therapy as a treatment approach to child abuse. *Child Psychiatry Quarterly* 21(4):191–198.

Piaget, J., and Inhelder, B. (1969). *The Psychology of the Child.* New York: Basic Books.

Putman, F. W., Helmers, K., and Trickett, P. K. (1993). Development, reliability, and validity of a child dissociation scale. *Child Abuse and Neglect* 17:731–741.

Riley, S. (1987). The advantages of art therapy in an outpatient clinic. *American Journal of Art Therapy* 26(1):21–29.

——— (1988). Adolescence and family art therapy: treating the "adolescent family" with family art therapy. *Art Therapy* 4:43–51.

——— (1993). Illustrating the family story: art therapy, a lens for viewing the family's reality. *The Arts in Psychotherapy* 20:1–12.

——— (1994). *Integrative Approaches to Family Art Therapy*. Chicago, IL: Magnolia Street.

Robbins, A. (1987). *The Artist as Therapist*. New York: Human Sciences Press.

Robbins, A., and Cooper, B. (1993). Resistance in art therapy: a multi-model approach to treatment. *Art Therapy: Journal of the American Art Therapy Association* 10(4):208–218.

Rubin, J. (1978). *Child Art Therapy*. New York: Van Nostrand Reinhold.

Salter, A., Richardson, C., and Martin, P. (1985). Treating abusive parents. *Child Welfare* 64(4):327–341.

Scharff, D. E. (1989). Young children and play in object relations family therapy. *Journal of Psychotherapy and the Family* 5(3–4):75–83.

Scharff, J. S., and Scharff, D. E. (1994). *Object Relations Therapy of Physical and Sexual Trauma*. Northvale, NJ: Jason Aronson.

Seinfeld, J. (1989). Therapy with a severely abused child: an object relations perspective. *Clinical Social Work Journal* 17(1):40–49.

Silver, R. A. (1990). *Silver Drawing Test of Cognitive Skills and Adjustment*. Florida: Ablin.

Sivan, A. B., Schor, D. P., Keoppl, G. K., and Noble, L. D. (1988). Interaction of normal children with anatomical dolls. *Child Abuse and Neglect* 12:295–304.

Sobol, B. S. (1982). Art therapy and strategic family therapy. *American Journal of Art Therapy* 21:43–52.

St. Clair, M. (1986). *Object Relations and Self Psychology: An Introduction.* Belmont, CA: Brooks/Cole.

Stanek, M. (1983). *Don't Hurt Me, Mama.* Niles, IL: Albert Whitman.

Steele, B. F., and Alexander, H. (1981). Long-term effects of sexual abuse in childhood. In *Sexually Abused Children and their Families,* ed. P. B. Mrazek and C. H. Kempe, pp. 223–233. Oxford: Pergamon.

Sussal, C. M. (1992). Object relations family therapy as a model for practice. *Clinical Social Work Journal* 20(3):313–321.

Terr, L. C. (1985). Children traumatized in small groups. In *Post-Traumatic Stress Disorder in Children,* ed. S. Eth and R. S. Pynoos, pp. 47–70. Washington DC: American Psychiatric Press.

———— (1990). *Too Scared to Cry: How Trauma Affects Children . . . and Ultimately Us All.* New York: Basic Books.

———— (1994). *Unchained Memories.* New York: Basic Books.

Tinnin, L. (1990). Biological processes in nonverbal communication and their role in the making and interpretation of art. *The American Journal of Art Therapy* 29:9–13.

Tuohy, A. L. (1987). Psychoanalytic perspectives on child abuse. *Child and Adolescent Social Work Journal* 4(1):25–40.

Ulman, E. (1977). A new use of art in psychiatic diagnosis. In *Art Therapy in Theory and Practice,* ed. E. Ulman and P. Dachinger, pp. 361–386. New York: Schocken.

van der Kolk, B. A. (1987). *Psychological Trauma.* Washington, DC: American Psychiatric Press.

———— (1994). The body keeps the score: memory and the evolving psychobiology of posttraumatic stress. *Harvard Review of Psychiatry* 1(5):253–265.

van der Kolk, B. A., and van der Hart, O. (1991). The intrusive past: the flexibility of memory and the engraving of trauma. *American Imago* 48(4):425–454.

Walker, L. E. A., ed. (1988). *Handbook of Sexual Abuse of Children: Assessment and Treatment Issues.* New York: Springer.

Will, D. (1983). Approaching the incestuous and sexually abusive family. *Journal of Adolescence* 6(3):229–246.

Wilson, J., and Lindy, J. (1994). Empathic strain and countertransference roles: case illustrations. In *Countertransference in Treatment of PTSD*, pp. 62–82. New York: Guilford.

Wilson, J., Lindy, J., and Raphael, B. (1994). Empathic strain and therapist defense: Type I and II CTRs. In *Countertransference in the Treatment of PTSD*, ed. J. Wilson and J. Lindy, pp. 31–61. New York: Guilford.

Index